LESSONS LEARNED
—— *on the* ——
AUDIT TRAIL

by

RICHARD F.
CHAMBERS

BEST WISHES MARY LYNN!

[signature]

SPONSORED BY

**The Institute of
Internal Auditors
Dallas Chapter**

The Institute of Internal Auditors
Research Foundation

"Richard draws from decades of experience to deliver a comprehensive playbook for anyone committed to becoming a successful leader in the internal audit profession."

Harold Silverman, CIA, CRMA, CPA, CISA
Vice President, Internal Audit
The Wendy's Company

"Following the passage of the Sarbanes-Oxley Act, internal auditors were proclaimed 'new rock stars' in the profession, but Richard Chambers is a 'legendary rock star.' Richard's gift to us all in this book is his ability to weave personal wisdom, stories, and insights about the profession, earned through real-life successes and disappointments. You will learn about what works and why so that you can curtail your learning curve and fast-track your career. As Richard says, 'The paradox of learning important lessons later in life is that you have less time to apply them.' This book is a road map for embarking on your own extraordinary internal audit trail."

Carolyn D. Saint
Vice President, Internal Audit
7-Eleven, Inc.

"Richard Chambers has been there and done that. Using real-life examples, he underscores themes of diligence, ethics, professionalism, and integrity. With experience comes wisdom, and the pages of *Lessons Learned on the Audit Trail* are brimming with both."

Dr. Joseph T. Wells, CFE, CPA
Founder and Chairman
Association of Certified Fraud Examiners

"Few internal auditors have interacted directly with the White House, testified before Congress, worked for four-star generals, and advised Fortune 500 boards of directors. In his book, Richard shares first-hand stories and many more in illustrating lessons that will benefit every internal auditor."

Maurice Gilbert
CEO
Corporate Compliance Insights

"Lessons Learned on the Audit Trail is a must-read for internal auditors at any stage in their career. Richard's forty-year journey in internal auditing is both compelling and inspirational."

Mike Gowell
Vice President and General Manager
TeamMate

"Richard has done a terrific job articulating powerful insights from his remarkable career. This book is essential not just for internal auditors, but for anyone concerned about the effective role of internal audit in organizational governance. I will use it to provide future internal auditors with special insights that go well beyond the technical standards."

Bob George
Lecturer
University of Texas at Austin
PwC Partner (Retired)

Published by The Institute of Internal Auditors Research Foundation
247 Maitland Avenue
Altamonte Springs, Florida 32701-4201

Cover photograph by Peter Burg/Burg Photographix

ISBN-13: 978-0-89413-903-1
19 18 17 16 15   RRD   2 3 4 5 6 7 8

DEDICATION

To Kim, Natalie, Christina, and Allison,
whose love and support were instrumental to any success
I might have had on the audit trail.

CONTENTS

FOREWORD

I first met Richard Chambers in 2003 when I traveled to Orlando, Florida, at the invitation of the late Bill Bishop, The Institute of Internal Auditors' (IIA's) president at the time. I can still recall discussing the extraordinary pressures facing the internal audit profession in the wake of the newly enacted U.S. Sarbanes-Oxley Act of 2002 and many of the other developments that had occurred in the previous year. At that time, neither Richard nor I could have imagined all the challenges and opportunities the profession would face in the coming decade. We have remained in contact since then, often comparing perspectives on developments in the profession we both love so well. I was pleased when I learned Richard returned to The IIA in 2009 as president and CEO, and have been excited about The IIA's growth and development under his leadership.

My career did not begin in internal audit. After working in public and corporate accounting for several years, I was offered a position in internal audit. The IIA helped get my new career off to a strong start, and I quickly began to think of internal audit as the best-kept secret in corporate America. I liked the challenge and diversity that internal audit provided and the ability to learn about so many different aspects of an organization.

Fueled by the efforts of The IIA, by the time I was vice president of internal audit at WorldCom, there had been tremendous transformation and growth in the profession. As the audit team for a company that employed some 100,000 people with more than $38 billion in annual revenue, internal auditors had to be quick studies. We were constantly thrust into new areas where the risks and challenges changed often.

When Richard shared with me that he was writing a book and asked me to write the Foreword, I was delighted to do so because I have often gleaned valuable insight from my conversations with him. In *Lessons Learned on the Audit Trail*, Richard shares his own journey of nearly forty years in the internal audit profession. I believe that his unique story will prove extremely valuable to both new and seasoned internal auditors around the world.

Throughout the book, Richard champions high professional standards and ethical conduct, and his passion for the internal audit profession comes through on every page. He shares often hard-won lessons learned while on the audit trail, and principles that can help you transform your career, take advantage of opportunities, and be well prepared for the challenges ahead.

The experiences Richard shares and the principles he recommends reveal the extraordinary opportunity for today's internal audit departments to provide immense value to the organizations they serve. Richard recognizes the unlimited potential of the internal audit professional to develop the skills and competencies required in an age with emerging challenges and risks.

I highly recommend *Lessons Learned on the Audit Trail*. Whether you are a young person considering the internal audit field for your career or a seasoned, experienced internal audit professional, you will find lessons and principles that can better equip you to meet the demands of this incredible profession and blaze your own trail.

—**Cynthia Cooper**
CEO, The CooperGroup LLC
Author, *Extraordinary Circumstances*

—— ACKNOWLEDGMENTS ——

Writing this book has been one of the most rewarding experiences of my life. However, it would not have been possible without the encouragement and support of so many members of my family, friends, and colleagues. Whether entertaining Army generals or cultivating and sustaining relationships with key IIA volunteers, my wife, Kim, has been a vital partner on the audit trail I discuss in this book. She has been encouraging me to write a book for as long as I can remember. Her words of advice, reassurance, patience, and understanding over the past few months were vital to delivering this manuscript. My father, Linville Chambers, was a lifelong source of inspiration personally and professionally. His death in 2013 was a catalyst for my own self-reflection and the decision to write this book. Thanks, Dad, for all you taught me about life, the pursuit of excellence, and perseverance. My mother, Mildred Chambers, has always been a pillar of strength. Without her loving support throughout my academic years and the early years of my career, there would likely have been no audit trail. My talented and beautiful daughters, Natalie McElwee, Christina Morton, and Allison Chambers, have always been unwavering in their affection and support. No matter how many times the new chapters in my professional journey disrupted their lives, their love and resilience always shined through.

Thank you to The IIA's Dallas Chapter for sponsorship of this IIA Research Foundation publication. Thanks to Lillian McAnally, my editor, whose expertise and time in organizing this project and polishing the manuscript was invaluable. Words cannot express my gratitude to Barbara Dycus, Jodi Swauger, Edward Popkins Jr., and

John Babinchak for the talent and enthusiasm they each brought to the editing process. Thanks also to Bill and Linda Michalisin for rolling up their sleeves to make sure the book cover would have the appropriate look and feel, and to Paula Michaels for her patience and perseverance in getting the appropriate image for the cover.

Thanks also to my former PwC colleagues, Gary Chamblee and Bob George, for taking time to review portions of the early manuscript. Their constructive advice and words of encouragement couldn't have come at a better time. In addition, I deeply appreciate the assistance of Lori Ondecker, Kevin Mayeux, Stacy Mantzaris, Don Sparks, Mike Gowell, Bob Shaw, and Karla Talleur, all of whom served as a sounding board at some point during the project for professional or technical advice—or simply helped me refresh my memory about events along the journey. Finally, thank you to my former colleague, Ronnie Ross, for her "eagle eye" review of the final manuscript.

For the Chinese edition of my book, I would like to thank the leadership of IIA Chinese Taiwan for their dedication and support throughout the translation and publishing process. I would like to specifically thank Doris Wang for her efforts in making this edition possible.

Finally, I would be remiss if I didn't thank the countless men and women whom I had the privilege of calling my colleagues in the Trust Company of Georgia, the U.S. Government Accountability Office, the U.S. Army, the U.S. Department of Health and Human Services, the U.S. Postal Service, TVA, PwC, and The IIA. The opportunity to work with such extraordinary professionals over the course of almost forty years has been the highest honor of my life. Without them, my audit trail would have been a lonely and unfulfilling path.

—— ABOUT THE AUTHOR ——

Richard F. Chambers, CIA, QIAL, CGAP, CCSA, CRMA, is president and CEO of The Institute of Internal Auditors (IIA), the global professional association for internal auditors. He has spent nearly forty years in internal auditing, serving as inspector general of the Tennessee Valley Authority, deputy inspector general of the U.S. Postal Service, and director of the U.S. Army Internal Review at the Pentagon. Before joining The IIA, he was national practice leader in Internal Audit Advisory Services at Pricewaterhouse-Coopers (PwC).

Richard is a prolific blogger and speaker and has been featured in numerous major media outlets, including *The Wall Street Journal, The New York Times,* Bloomberg Radio, and CNBC. *Accounting Today* selected him as one of the 100 Most Influential People in Accounting, and the National Association of Corporate Directors (NACD) named him one of the most influential leaders in corporate governance. Richard and his wife, Kim, reside in the Orlando, Florida, area and have three grown daughters, Natalie, Christina, and Allison.

Lessons Along the Way

The Merriam-Webster Dictionary defines an audit trail as *"a record of a sequence of events from which a history may be reconstructed."*[1] As I reflect on my own career in internal auditing, I often contemplate the sequence of events that brought me to where I am today. More important than the events themselves, however, are the lessons I have learned along my personal audit trail.

For some time, friends and colleagues have encouraged me to write about my career and the lessons I've learned. For the past five years, I have been sharing many of my experiences in speeches and lectures around the world and in the blog I maintain for The Institute of Internal Auditors (The IIA). The reaction from audiences and blog readers to the real-life experiences I use to illustrate my professional challenges and opportunities has been very gratifying. But I never really felt the timing was right to share my experiences in the more-extended format of a book—until now.

My journey on the audit trail has spanned nearly forty years and given me the opportunity to work for a diverse group of organizations and with immensely talented individuals, and it has taken me to all corners of the globe.

Along the way, I learned valuable lessons about the profession, those we serve, and life in general. In this book, I share the most important of these lessons and experiences to demonstrate the exciting potential internal auditing holds for those seeking a life of passion and "living color" in a profession many people view as a dull, black-and-white undertaking.

It is important for you, as you read this book, to be aware that it does not constitute guidance from The IIA. While in my view the guidance I share is clearly aligned with the current International Professional Practices Framework (IPPF), it should not be used as a substitute for that framework, and I am not endeavoring to give you direction or guidance as you manage an internal audit department or undertake internal audit engagements. Every internal audit department is different, and every set of circumstances is different. This book is a composite view of organizations I have worked in, led, or dealt with throughout my career, and these are my personal views about how best to address some of the challenges we face in this important profession.

In sharing my experiences and exploring how the lessons I learned apply to internal auditing today, I frequently draw on my time spent in government. Because government operations are generally more transparent than those in the corporate sector, I am able to talk more candidly about the details, referring to real people, dates, and locations. Having spent portions of my career in government, the corporate world, and the not-for-profit sector, I find the similarities far outweigh the differences. As you partake of my experiences, I strongly suspect you will agree.

Internal auditing can be an extraordinarily rewarding profession, giving one a sense of accomplishment unlike any other. It has been that way for me, and I believe that, as you explore with me the lessons I have learned, you will unearth important principles that can make your personal internal audit journey equally rewarding. My hope is that, as you read this, you will learn how to harness your personal passion for the profession and live your life in color, not in black and white.

I want to begin by inviting you into my life, so you can see how certain circumstances and opportunities prepared me to find success on my personal audit trail.

—Richard F. Chambers, CIA, QIAL, CGAP, CCSA, CRMA
President and CEO, The Institute of Internal Auditors

A Bird's-Eye View
of the Audit Trail

As we travel down life's path, each of us experiences things in both our personal and professional lives that prepare us for the challenges and opportunities that lie ahead. In that regard, my journey is not unique.

What does set mine apart in this day and age is that I have spent almost four decades serving the same profession—internal auditing. Over the course of my career, I have learned many important lessons, some early in my career and some much later. The paradox of learning important lessons later in life is that you have less time to apply them, which was a motivating factor for me in writing this book. If I can help just one internal auditor to be better prepared for the challenges and opportunities that lie ahead in his or her career, then the effort will have been worth it.

Before diving headlong into the lessons learned, it might help to put some of my experiences and milestones into perspective by dedicating a few pages to a quick chronological review of my career. So I begin with a bird's-eye view of my audit trail and how it has shaped my personal philosophy.

A Simple Legacy

My father came from humble beginnings. His formal education was limited, yet he achieved remarkable things. He grew up in a family of six children and had to drop out of high school before graduating to help with the family farm and business, but he went on to secure a comfortable living as a civil service employee with the U.S. Army where he did extremely well. My dad was an extraordinary influence in my life, and it was he who taught me one of my earliest lessons.

He passed away in June 2013, and as I reflected on his life in the months that followed, I realized what an incredible number of people respected him, trusted him, believed in him, and even revered him.

LIFE LESSON #1

You measure success not by where you ultimately arrive,
but by the journey from where you started.

My dad was serving in the Army when I was born in the hospital at Fort McClellan in Alabama. We lived there until I was about to enter sixth grade and my father transferred to the U.S. Army Reserve Personnel Command in St. Louis, Missouri. The schools in Alabama were far behind those I attended in St. Louis, and for the six years we lived there, I always felt as if I was struggling to catch up to the others in my class. Still, those were very formative, memorable years.

At the end of my junior year of high school, we moved back south to Atlanta, Georgia. By then I had caught up with my school peers in St. Louis and no longer felt inferior or disadvantaged. The schools in Atlanta were significantly behind those in St. Louis, and suddenly I felt incredibly liberated—I was being taught information in twelfth grade that I had first encountered in ninth grade. That senior year of high school was great for my self-confidence and a great launch pad for going to college.

My father was still in civil service, as was my mother; both worked at Fort McPherson in Atlanta. I knew they could not afford to send me out of state to college, so I attended Georgia State University in Atlanta. I started in the business school without a major and with modest expectations for myself, but I hit the ground running and did well. I made the dean's list my first semester and never looked back.

Finding My Way On to the Trail

As a Georgia State freshman in 1972, I knew only that I wanted a degree in business. But when I took my first accounting course, during my sophomore year, I was surprised by how well I did—and how much I enjoyed it. I took a second course, also did well, and decided to major in accounting.

I also secured a part-time job at First National Bank of Atlanta, just two blocks from school. I started in the check processing department but, as my appreciation for my new major grew, I transferred to the accounting department. I became so intensely involved with accounting that I finished my four-year degree in just two years and nine months.

A Career Is Launched

I wanted to go right on and earn a master's in business administration at Georgia State. I also wanted to continue working close to school, so when an opportunity came up in the internal audit department of Atlanta-based Trust Company of Georgia, I took it even though I had no deep understanding of what internal auditing was. My first year as an internal auditor was a great learning experience, and I made some great friends.

I had also applied after college for a government job in the federal General Accounting Office (GAO), but in 1975, the nation was in the throes of a recession and no openings were available. A year later, however, a letter from the GAO arrived in the mail—not inviting me for an interview but offering me a job! It was a great opportunity. My parents were excited, and I was, too, though I was also a little nervous about moving so far from home and leaving in the middle of my MBA program. Still, I packed my belongings and joined the GAO's international division in Washington, DC.

It was an incredible experience for many reasons. It taught me a lot about the importance of family and friends, even when you are separated from them by great distances. The work was interesting, and I learned a lot working for Dr. Eleanor Hadley, who had served on Gen. Douglas MacArthur's staff as it helped rebuild Japan's economy after World War II. Now with the GAO, she was an economist leading an important audit project for the agency—another important lesson for me.

My stay in Hadley's office turned out to be a short one, however. The GAO announced that it had hired too many people for headquarters so it offered all of those it had hired that year a chance to work in one of its branch offices, Atlanta among them. Also, I had received an offer to interview for a job in the Internal Review Division of the U.S. Army Forces Command (FORSCOM) headquartered in Atlanta. The Army had internal review offices in virtually every one of its installations and facilities around the world; they were local commanders' internal auditors much as a CEO has his or her own internal audit function in the corporate sector.

LIFE LESSON #2

You don't have to be a classically and professionally trained internal auditor to successfully lead audit teams.

I had come to the fork in the road that everyone encounters at some point in their career. In my case, it was a three-pronged fork: I could stay in Washington, the least favorable option for me personally. I could go back to Atlanta to work for the GAO at a higher level, as a GS7 grade employee. Or I could return to Atlanta to work in FORSCOM Internal Review—a GS5 position. At that point in my career, my best option might have been to go for the higher pay grade. But the GAO job in Atlanta would be 90 percent travel, and that would have meant I couldn't return to my MBA program. So instead I said, "I'm going to work for the Army."

Working for Uncle Sam

I joined FORSCOM's Internal Review Office in November 1976. FORSCOM was one of the largest commands in the entire U.S. Department of Defense, responsible for all Army bases in the United States, Panama, and Puerto Rico.

I moved quickly through a three-year internship. I felt pretty good about the training and began to believe that my destiny lay in internal auditing. I remember meeting with the deputy controller a year or so after I was hired. He was a full colonel, kind of a gruff guy, and he asked, "Well, what is your career goal?"

I said, "I'd like to be the Chief of Internal Review here."

And he said, "Oh, yeah? How long do you think it will take you to reach that level?"

"Oh, I don't know," I said. "I would imagine it would be fifteen years," which was pretty presumptuous—just fifteen years to move from a GS5 employee to the command's GS14 head of internal review.

After talking with the colonel, I remember going back to my boss, Bernie Shell, who asked, "What did the deputy controller ask you?"

I had the kind of relationship with him where I could be direct, so I said, "He asked me what I wanted to do with my career."

Bernie asked, "What did you tell him?"

And I said, "I told him I want your job."

"Oh, yeah?" he said with a smile, "How long do you think that will take?"

I said, "I told him it would take fifteen years."

He said, "Well, that's a little ambitious. But that's probably about when I'll be ready to retire."

As it turns out, I did it in eleven years. But not without a couple of detours first.

In early 1980, I received a letter from another federal agency offering me a promotion. By that time, the Army had moved me from GS5 through GS7 and GS9 to GS11. But now the U.S. Department of Health and Human Services in Atlanta was offering me a job in its Bureau of Medicare as a GS12.

I was smitten with the idea of making GS12, so I jumped at the opportunity. I left Fort McPherson and shifted to downtown Atlanta to work in the Bureau of Medicare as an accountant with auditor-like responsibilities. It was a desk job, pouring over financial reports sent to the bureau by hospitals seeking reimbursements.

I was bored. While it was close to internal auditing, it was extremely tedious work. I missed the variety of responsibilities in my work at Fort McPherson, where I had been able to assess internal review departments as far away as Panama—something most auditors don't get a chance to do until much later in their careers.

I had kept in contact with Bernie back at FORSCOM, so after a few months with Medicare I asked him, "What would you think if I wanted to come back?"

"You'd have to come back as a GS11," he said, "because I can't bring you back as a 12."

I said, "Well, I'd understand that." So little more than a year after leaving Fort McPherson, I returned to FORSCOM Internal Review. And I had learned another lesson, one I would struggle with more than once in my career.

LIFE LESSON #3

Be careful what you wish for. There's more to a career than the next raise or promotion; make sure that next job is something you truly want to do.

I stayed in FORSCOM Internal Review this time from 1981 to 1984 and was promoted back to GS12. But in the meantime, a guy named Joe Plunkett, whom I had known from my early days in the command, had moved up to head FORSCOM's cost analysis division, which was staffed with operations research analysts whose expertise required a deep background in mathematics. Joe offered me an opportunity to work in a completely different discipline than internal auditing.

This time, I sat down and did something my dad had taught me years earlier. I created a list of pros and cons for taking or not taking the job. One thing that appealed to me was the pay-rate structure, which was light years ahead of internal review's. In cost analysis, GS13s did regular work, while in internal review you had to be a manager to be a GS13.

But that's not what cinched the deal in my mind. I had written an audit report that was pretty critical of certain operations, but Bernie had left it sitting on his desk for months, reluctant to send it out. So I finally decided, "I'm not happy if I can't do the work I need to do." I went in to see Bernie and said, "I hate to do this to you, but I've decided I'm going to go and do this other work."

I knew he was disappointed. "I'm not going to bring you back again," he said.

"I won't ask," I told him.

"Why are you doing this?" he asked.

"I feel I need to grow and do other things," I said. "And, frankly, I'm really disappointed because this audit report I wrote has sat here for months, and I feel like you are not going to issue it because it somehow is going to stir up too much heat."

Stretching Opportunities

I began working in the cost analysis division in February 1984. I suddenly found myself surrounded by some very smart, very talented people. You had to have twenty-four semester hours of college-level math to work in that division; the only reason I had qualified was because I had both an undergraduate degree and an MBA.

Working in cost analysis also taught me a lot about how internal auditing is viewed by others. My new colleagues teased me unmercifully about being an auditor, suggesting I had come over to them from "the dark side." Despite the teasing, I grew to enjoy the cost analysis work and made lifelong friends during my tenure.

Sometime in late 1987 or early 1988, the command's deputy controller, who by that time was a civilian, not a military officer, informed me that Bernie Shell was going to retire. He said the command's chief of staff, Maj. Gen. Robert Wiegand, was getting ready to recruit a new Chief of Internal Review—and the brigadier general controller had recommended me for the position.

I was surprised and excited but conflicted. I knew the person who had been Bernie's deputy for many years wanted the job, and he was a close friend who had mentored me and treated me like one of his family. And I was only thirty-three years old; the thought of being the chief of FORSCOM Internal Review, with seventy offices and 300 auditors, was a bit intimidating.

A few months later, the selection committee announced my appointment. It was a huge opportunity; I reported directly to the chief of staff, which put me on the "personal staff" of a four-star general—the Army's highest-ranking officer. I remember that, at my first meeting with Gen. Wiegand, his executive officer asked, "How old are you?" He couldn't believe they had picked somebody so young for the job.

My first year as Chief of Internal Review was one of the most exhilarating of my life. I was fortunate to have an outstanding deputy, Bob Shaw, and I quickly garnered the support of senior military officials throughout the command. Gen. Wiegand was ecstatic; he felt that the internal review office had suddenly flourished on his watch. When I completed some routine personnel paperwork a year after assuming my new role, the general became alarmed that I might leave. He quickly directed personnel officials to promote me to a GS15—the highest grade in the GS system. I certainly was not going to argue with him, so I became one of the youngest GS15s in the Army at barely thirty-four years of age. It was the summer of 1989.

Opportunities and Challenges

That July, I married a young lady named Kim. Little did I appreciate at the time how important my companion would be as I navigated the peaks and valleys that lay ahead. She has been my mate now for almost twenty-five years, and together we have raised three beautiful daughters who are each pursuing their own trail in life.

A couple of years after Kim and I married, I entered the U.S. Army War College. The name is a bit of a misnomer, because it's not designed to train people for fighting wars—it's more of a graduate-level program designed to prepare the next generation of senior Army leaders for the strategic challenges they and the military may face. When I was notified in the fall of 1990 that I had been selected to attend the year-long program, it was admitting about 300 students a year—including only six civilians.

The Army was already beginning to dramatically downsize in response to the end of the Cold War with the Soviet Union. I wrote two or three papers at the Army War College that focused on the ramifications of downsizing the military's internal audit force. My message was "pay now and pay later." Various commanders were cutting back on internal review in an attempt to save money, but in doing so they were divesting the Army of resources that could help it save money later. The situation was similar to that of a farmer who eats his seed corn; if you eat the seed corn, you will have nothing to plant later on. My message had an effect on certain leaders at the Pentagon.

Upon moving back to Atlanta in the summer of 1992 and returning to FORSCOM, I began to feel as if I had achieved all I could at the giant Army command. Further advancement was unlikely; I was already a GS15, and there were no audit positions in FORSCOM with a pay grade higher than mine. But then I began getting over-tures from senior officials in the Office of the Assistant Secretary of the Army for Financial Management. That would mean a lateral move to Washington, and I knew the cost of living was much higher in the DC area than it was in Atlanta. "Why would I do that to my family?" I thought. When I didn't answer the Pentagon right away, the Army's principal deputy assistant secretary of the Army for financial management, Neil Ginnetti, finally contacted me and said, "If you don't do this, I'll just assume that you are telling us that you don't want any further career advancement."

Another promotion at FORSCOM was unlikely—there was only one Senior Executive Service (SES) position for which I might qual-ify. And I had seventeen years left before I could retire from the Army with full benefits. "Maybe I ought to do it," I thought.

So I went to work at the Pentagon right after Labor Day in 1993. As the Army's director of internal review, my immediate boss was a guy named Ernie Gregory, one of the most charismatic leaders I have ever known. With Ernie and Neil supporting me, I felt very good about the move to Washington.

Even after the downsizing of the previous four years, the Army still boasted more than 1,400 internal review auditors in more than 300 offices around the world. The responsibilities of my new job were enormous. During my years at the Pentagon, I was not only the direc-tor of internal review but also the person charged with oversight of the Army's internal controls and financial reporting programs. Once again, I was fortunate to have outstanding deputies (Bill O'Hare and Bob Barnhart), without whom I would have never succeeded.

But around the Army, the next career move is often more about waiting your turn than anything else. I was still in my early 40s and didn't want to labor year after year doing the same things—espe-cially at a time when others were working tirelessly to divert internal review's resources to their departments. The Pentagon was a great experience, and I am extremely proud of all that we accomplished in internal review, but we also spent much of our time holding the fort against what seemed like an endless series of budgetary assaults, which I will discuss in a later chapter.

LIFE LESSON #4

That which does not kill us may or may not make us stronger, but regular bouts of adversity build your inner strength.

In early 1997, I attended a five-week leadership development course at the Federal Executive Institute in Charlottesville, Virginia, that emphasized personal as well as professional growth. During the course, I began to think, "I've been with the Army for twenty-one years, but I didn't sign a lifelong contract. Washington is full of rich opportunities for growth and advancement."

Congress a year earlier had passed an amendment to the Inspector General Act creating an inspector general (IG) position within the U.S. Postal Service (USPS). The USPS Board of Directors then hired its first IG—Karla Corcoran—who was determined to build an organization with the resources and capabilities worthy of the agency. I applied for an executive-level position with the Postal Service's Office of the Inspector General, though that application didn't go anywhere.

The same year the Postal Service got an IG, I had developed a course on quick response auditing that I taught on behalf of the U.S. Government Audit Training Institute. When I did the class in the fall of 1997, someone who knew Karla attended and afterward told her, "This is somebody you should look at." A couple of days later, I heard from the IG's human resources department and went for an interview. Soon after, I was offered a job with the Postal Service Office of the Inspector General (OIG).

After twenty-one years with the Army, I left the Pentagon in February 1998 and moved a short distance up the Potomac River to Rosslyn, Virginia, where the Postal Service's IG office was located.

The first morning was spent in an orientation attended by a lot of other people, because this was a period of incredible growth for the operation, which in three years would grow from nothing to a staff of more than 500 people.

I was hired as the deputy assistant inspector general for audit. As I sat in the orientation, Karla, who had come in to address everyone briefly, saw me and said, "I need to borrow you." I left the orientation and followed her next door, where a team was in the process of editing an audit report. Like many new organizations, the Postal Service's OIG was working hard to perfect its processes, and audit report writing was at the top of Karla's list of priorities.

Later in the book I talk about some of the USPS processes I helped implement to make the audit reporting more effective and efficient. Karla was trying to build an organization within the USPS based on values known as TLC3—short for teamwork, leadership, creativity, communication, and conceptualization. It took me a while to figure out how I could leverage my classically based internal audit background in a TLC3 environment, but once I did, I moved up rapidly in the organization. I was promoted to assistant IG for audit in 1999 and to deputy IG in 2000. In the process, I became Karla's right arm for audit matters, attending audit committee meetings with her and twice going with her to brief Congress. I helped her testify on both occasions by answering congressional questions about our audits.

A Position of Influence

My successes within the Postal Service OIG had been noticed by Ned McWherter, a member of the USPS Board of Governors and chairman of its audit committee. A former governor of Tennessee, McWherter began to talk to me in early 2000 about going to the Tennessee Valley Authority (TVA) as its inspector general. TVA was in the midst of a huge public feud, with the agency's board chairman accusing its IG of ethical misconduct. This was all over the news, and TVA officials were looking for someone who could serve as IG on an interim basis while the charges were investigated.

That February, when I told Karla that I wanted to consider the interim opportunity at TVA, she was very supportive, though the opportunity evaporated a month later when the FBI cleared the TVA inspector general of any misconduct and he resumed his duties. But then that summer, I got a call from TVA asking me to come to Knoxville, Tennessee, because the IG was going to announce his retirement—and they wanted me to take the job. TVA's Board of Directors interviewed me and offered the job, which I accepted.

TVA is the largest producer of wholesale electricity in the United States and one of the largest utility companies in the world, with nuclear, coal, and hydroelectric generating capabilities. I had a staff of about ninety people, half of them auditors and half criminal investigators. The IG post carried a lot of authority, including subpoena powers, because Congress had set up the federal government's IGs to function as independent watchdogs of their agencies.

Part of the fallout from the feud between the prior IG and the TVA chairman was a bill in Congress to make the agency's IG post a presidential appointment. It was approved by lawmakers in December 2000 as part of a larger piece of legislation.

I assumed my tenure at TVA was now limited to however long it took the newly elected president, George W. Bush, to appoint a successor. By that time I had twenty-four and a half years of civil service—but needed twenty-five to retire with an immediate pension. I just needed to get to August 1, 2001.

I never felt as if I had a really good relationship with TVA management or its board. Because of media coverage of the earlier controversy, media reports on audits we issued during my tenure, and the IG's statutory independence, TVA board members seemed very suspicious of anything I did that might create public turmoil. But apparently I made a better impression outside the agency. I met with members of Congress monthly to brief them on TVA matters, and with TVA operating in seven states, there were fourteen senators and twenty-eight House members on Capitol Hill whom I considered key stakeholders. In July, I received a call from the U.S. Office of Presidential Personnel and figured the president was going to appoint somebody as TVA's new IG. Only two weeks remained until my retirement threshold, so I wasn't terribly concerned about the timing of that, but then the person calling me said, "The president has decided to make his appointment at TVA, and he would like to appoint you. Would you be interested?"

I was quite flattered by the offer, but I was also deeply conflicted. A presidential appointment as IG is quite prestigious, but it also has its drawbacks, and I was in the unique position of having more than one option. Initially, I said I was interested in the appointment, which triggered the task of conducting background investigations. The executive branch would not even announce a nomination until those checks were complete.

As the background investigation was underway, I began exploring other career options. I had been actively involved in The Institute of Internal Auditors (The IIA) for some years. I had served on the Government Relations Committee and was now on the International Internal Auditing Standards Board, becoming its chairman in 2000. Bill Bishop, The IIA's CEO at the time, had already been pressing me to accept an executive position with the Florida-based organization once I retired from TVA. Bill's persuasive powers finally convinced me to make the tough decision on my career path only days before the background investigation was slated for completion.

When the White House called in early September to say, "You have cleared the background investigation, and we are going to announce your formal nomination for confirmation by the U.S. Senate at the press briefing tomorrow," I had to tell them, "I'm not going to take the job. I am withdrawing my name, and I'm going to retire from civil service." For one thing, if a new president was elected in 2004, I could be asked for my resignation at a time I had two children in college, and I simply did not want to labor under that kind of uncertainty. Also, I would not be eligible for any bonuses at TVA and could no longer do any outside work if I accepted the offer, which would mean giving up my teaching assignments at the Government Audit Training Institute. Many people at the time could not believe that I was passing up an opportunity to serve as a presidential appointee, but I have never regretted my decision.

Joining The IIA

Bill Bishop asked me to join The IIA as vice president of the Learning Center, with oversight of all the training, education, and certification programs as well as The IIA Research Foundation and bookstore. We left Knoxville and moved to Orlando, Florida. I had never run an operation in which I had to make money for the company, but under Bill's extraordinary tutelage, I learned quickly. I initiated a swift analysis of what worked and what didn't in the training and education arena.

Improvements included making great strides in identifying and delivering services to meet IIA member expectations. A few weeks after my arrival, WorldCom went under and The IIA became the epicenter of internal audit activity. Congress passed the U.S. Sarbanes-Oxley Act of 2002, and The IIA's membership and revenue went through the roof.

Bill began working on his plans to retire in 2004. He had been at The IIA since 1992, following his own extraordinary career in internal auditing. He definitely deserved to enjoy his golden years with his lovely wife, Mary. He made a couple of long, global trips in early 2004, flying back from Africa on March 6. He arrived back on Saturday, and I tried to reach him all the next day to tell him that our annual General Audit Management Conference was sold out for the first time ever.

But that same Sunday, I got a call from Mary, who told me Bill had suffered a massive heart attack and died. I was devastated. Receiving such news would affect not only me personally and professionally, but also the entire IIA organization. The IIA chairman of the board at the time asked me to become the acting president; a few days later, the board interviewed three candidates for the position, myself included. When I learned I had not been chosen as Bill's successor, I decided it was an opportunity to once again do something different, so I had conversations with the internal audit practice leaders of several of the accounting firms and major service providers. To my surprise, I received offers from four of them, including PricewaterhouseCoopers (PwC). PwC appealed most to me because I knew more people there and it would mean a move back to Atlanta.

I left The IIA in August 2004 but didn't want to sever my ties to the organization, so a year later I was back as a volunteer, serving as head of the International Conference Committee. After three years, I became chairman of the North American Board.

Navigating the Corporate Sector

My years at PwC were among the most amazing of my life. Unlike the newly minted accounting graduates who join a public accounting firm in their twenties, I had just turned fifty. I was surrounded by bright, young, and energetic professionals—some young enough to be my children. I was determined they would not outpace me, and I worked harder and longer during my PwC years than I had ever worked in my life. One of my first opportunities at PwC was helping the firm's general auditor, Gary Chamblee, a partner in the firm, run its internal audit function. It was a great opportunity for me to leverage my process design and implementation experiences from the Army and the Postal Service. In addition to that internal role, I was helping serve clients and write PwC's internal audit thought leadership. There were several dozen internal audit partners in the firm at the time, and I had the opportunity to work with each of them during my tenure there.

Dick Anderson, the national practice leader for PwC's internal audit advisory services, retired during my third year with the firm, and I was asked to take on his role. By that time I had been promoted to managing director and had won the trust and confidence of the internal audit leadership. In my new role, I became a "road warrior," traveling throughout the country in support of the practice.

While my first two years at PwC were extraordinarily rewarding for me professionally, being back in Atlanta was not as enjoyable. During our eleven-year absence, the population had grown by 40 percent, and the area's traffic and culture had changed dramatically. So when PwC's internal audit leader told me in early 2006 that I could live wherever I wanted, given my national role with the firm, I moved the family back to Orlando.

The mid-2000s were extraordinary years to be an internal auditor in the U.S. corporate sector. Implementation of Sarbanes-Oxley was underway, and resources were plentiful. During my tenure at PwC, I had the opportunity to work or interact with the internal audit departments of seventy-five U.S. Fortune 500 companies. Although disappointed when I was not selected as The IIA's CEO in 2004, I would never trade my years at PwC for anything. I had the support of great PwC partners such as Jim LaTorre and Dennis Bartolucci, and I learned more in those five years about client service, the corporate sector, business acumen, and sustaining a high performance culture than I had during the first twenty-nine years of my career.

LIFE LESSON #5

Disappointment and defeat build character.

Despite my experience with The IIA in 2004, I remained loyal to the organization because of all it had done for me over the years. In 2007–2008, as the boom in Sarbanes-Oxley resources started to wane and the nation's economy started to come apart, The IIA—like many other companies—faced extraordinary challenges. Despite my love for the work at PwC, I felt it my duty to make myself available when The IIA initiated a search for a new chief executive in late 2008. I was hired as CEO and president at the beginning of 2009—the depths of the Great Recession. Having been on the IIA board the year before, I knew the challenges I faced. March 2009 was the low point; working with an extraordinary team and with the support of a strong board of directors, I took the organization through a process of downsizing and reorganization designed to position us for recovery and to better serve the profession in the years ahead.

We have been on an incredible journey ever since. We began launching new initiatives—the Audit Executive Center, the Certification in Risk Management Assurance, the Audit Channel, and the American Center for Government Auditing, among others. We have set new records for membership, conference attendance and the number of global institutes, and we have quadrupled the organization's net worth. Today, we have the resources and talent at The IIA to serve our global membership in ways we never thought possible.

And we are well-positioned as a profession to tackle the challenges now before us. Internal audit departments continue to receive added resources, a reflection of greater realization of the value they provide by their key stakeholders. At the same time, audit plans reflect the growing velocity of regulatory compliance. Of course, there remain areas of opportunity—internal audit's role in addressing strategic business risks, in particular.

While I do not yet know if The IIA will be the last stop on my audit trail, it has certainly enabled me to pull together and draw upon all of the lessons learned during my other stops along the way. In the remaining chapters of this book, I will share many of those lessons and the circumstances that enabled me to get the most from them. I hope you find the journey worth your while.

Richard Chambers
Biographical Timeline

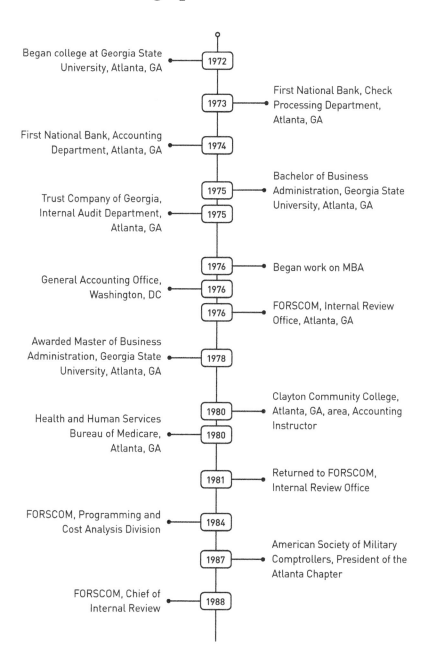

Began college at Georgia State
University, Atlanta, GA — **1972**

1973 — First National Bank, Check
Processing Department,
Atlanta, GA

First National Bank, Accounting
Department, Atlanta, GA — **1974**

1975 — Bachelor of Business
Administration, Georgia State
University, Atlanta, GA

Trust Company of Georgia,
Internal Audit Department, — **1975**
Atlanta, GA

1976 — Began work on MBA

General Accounting Office,
Washington, DC — **1976**

1976 — FORSCOM, Internal Review
Office, Atlanta, GA

Awarded Master of Business
Administration, Georgia State — **1978**
University, Atlanta, GA

1980 — Clayton Community College,
Atlanta, GA, area, Accounting
Instructor

Health and Human Services
Bureau of Medicare, — **1980**
Atlanta, GA

1981 — Returned to FORSCOM,
Internal Review Office

FORSCOM, Programming and
Cost Analysis Division — **1984**

1987 — American Society of Military
Comptrollers, President of the
Atlanta Chapter

FORSCOM, Chief of
Internal Review — **1988**

LESSONS LEARNED *on the* AUDIT TRAIL

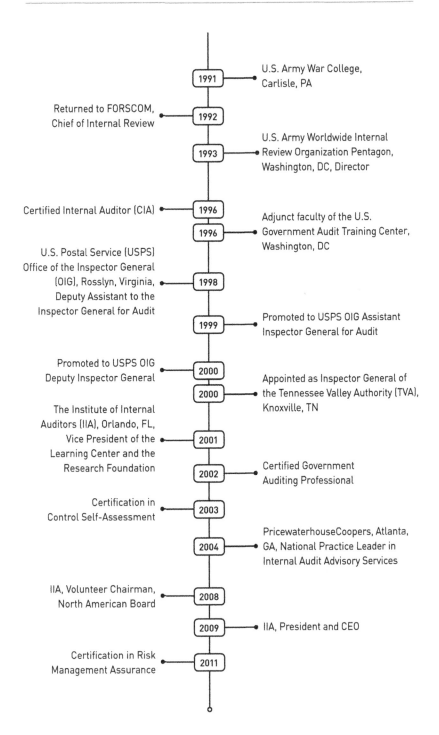

1991 — U.S. Army War College, Carlisle, PA

Returned to FORSCOM, Chief of Internal Review — **1992**

1993 — U.S. Army Worldwide Internal Review Organization Pentagon, Washington, DC, Director

Certified Internal Auditor (CIA) — **1996**

1996 — Adjunct faculty of the U.S. Government Audit Training Center, Washington, DC

U.S. Postal Service (USPS) Office of the Inspector General (OIG), Rosslyn, Virginia, Deputy Assistant to the Inspector General for Audit — **1998**

1999 — Promoted to USPS OIG Assistant Inspector General for Audit

Promoted to USPS OIG Deputy Inspector General — **2000**

2000 — Appointed as Inspector General of the Tennessee Valley Authority (TVA), Knoxville, TN

The Institute of Internal Auditors (IIA), Orlando, FL, Vice President of the Learning Center and the Research Foundation — **2001**

2002 — Certified Government Auditing Professional

Certification in Control Self-Assessment — **2003**

2004 — PricewaterhouseCoopers, Atlanta, GA, National Practice Leader in Internal Audit Advisory Services

IIA, Volunteer Chairman, North American Board — **2008**

2009 — IIA, President and CEO

Certification in Risk Management Assurance — **2011**

CHAPTER 2

Common Traits of Outstanding Internal Auditors

If you are going to succeed in the internal audit profession, not only must you pursue excellence on an ongoing basis, you must also exemplify certain core characteristics. Developing these attributes must be at the forefront of your mind, because it's a process that takes time. Eventually, you will exceed even your expectations if you continually pursue excellence.

I learned that lesson during my time at U.S. Army Forces Command headquarters in Atlanta. When I returned to FORSCOM Internal Review in March 1981, following my "not-so-excellent adventure" with the U.S. Department of Health and Human Services, I was surprised to learn that I was not the only new employee joining the department that week.

My boss, Bernie Shell, had also recruited a young certified public accountant (CPA) to join the staff—quite a coup for the unit.

It didn't take me long to realize that Bernie was quite smitten by my new colleague's CPA qualifications. A few months after we had both joined the staff, a huge opportunity arose to be a part of an audit team on an important engagement in Southern California. During my first stint at FORSCOM, I would have certainly been on the engagement team, but this time Bernie selected my colleague instead. When I expressed disappointment, Bernie said he needed my colleague's CPA credential to enhance the team's stature.

I thought Bernie's reasoning was flawed—the audit in question was focused mainly on operational, not financial, risks—and while I was disappointed, I wasn't defeated. I held my head high and supported the engagement team from FORSCOM headquarters in every way I could. I redoubled my efforts and took every opportunity to demonstrate the characteristics that had served me so well thus far in my career—hard work, passion, courage, dependability, and so on. It didn't take Bernie long to realize I was the one he really needed on the team; within a few months, my colleague and I switched roles, and I spent the next several months on the engagement.

What I learned from this experience was that, while certifications and qualifications are an important means of demonstrating proficiency, they are no substitute for the traits and attributes shared by truly successful internal auditors.

LIFE LESSON #6

Be willing to commit yourself to absolute excellence.
Don't settle for simply being good;
pursue greatness in everything you do.

Having spent nearly forty years in this profession, I've had the chance to interact with many exceptionally talented individuals from all sectors and industries, and I have observed that certain traits are common among the truly outstanding performers—the most talented, the absolute cream of the crop.

Characteristics of Success for Internal Auditors

If I were given the opportunity to build a brand new internal audit department tomorrow, there are five key characteristics that I would look for in every internal auditor I interviewed:

1. INTEGRITY AND COURAGE

For me, integrity, followed by courage, are paramount for any internal auditor. If you are not honest and fair with people, or not willing to go to bat for someone when honesty and fairness are at stake, you'll have a very difficult time getting others to listen to you or accept your work. Personal integrity is really that must-have trait. Some who have served in the internal audit profession haven't always demonstrated integrity (see chapter 14, "No One Is Immune to Ethical Lapses"), but in my experience, the vast majority of those in internal auditing are people of integrity.

The higher you go during a career in internal auditing, the more important it becomes to have a reputation for unflinching integrity and ethical behavior. The chief audit executive (CAE) has to be willing to go out on a limb as part of an organization's collective conscience. I can recall instances in my own career when, as the chief auditor, I have had to call out others because of their actions or behavior. For me, courage means being proactive and standing up for what you believe is right.

During my years at the Pentagon as director of internal review for the Army, I fought what I have come to call *the audit wars*. The U.S. Army Audit Agency (USAAA) and its head, the auditor general, had real designs on the internal review resources in the Army. While the USAAA had about 700 auditors on its staff, more than 1,000 internal review personnel around the world were organized as internal audit elements within their own organizations. The auditor general wanted that internal review staff, spread throughout the Army, to report to him. From 1994 almost until I left the Pentagon in 1998, it seemed a constant battle. The auditor general tried almost everything, and even convinced my old command at FORSCOM to let him run the audit function there.

I have always suspected that, while his initial plan would have been to have the internal review staff report directly to him as a group, he eventually would have consolidated the various operations with his own resources, depriving Army commanders around the globe of a vital form of oversight and troubleshooting, a resource they had possessed since World War II.

So strongly did we believe in the merits of the existing system that we persuaded the Assistant Secretary of the Army to agree to a test. Several internal review sites would operate as they always had, while an equal number would operate under the direction of the auditor general. Various metrics would be tracked during the test period to compare the two approaches in terms of how each one performed, what it achieved, what it cost to operate, and what it saved the Army.

Everyone agreed to the rules, and we began the test. When we compared the results at the end of the test period, the internal review model had clearly outperformed the USAAA-run sites. I wasn't surprised by this, because I knew the centralized USAAA would have difficulties matching the responsiveness and agility of the individual internal review sites, and over the year I had noted that it frequently took USAAA a year or more to finish an audit and publish a report.

Still, those years were a very stressful time for me. The auditor general was persistent in his attempts to take over internal review. He was essentially the equivalent of a three-star general and, as such, significantly outranked me. However, I knew—and so did he—that I was working for people who outranked him. And thanks to the support of people like Neil Ginnetti and Ernie Gregory, and the results of our "put up or shut up test," internal review still exists in the Army today, almost twenty years after *the audit wars.*

CAEs in the current economy face similar challenges. In the wake of the Great Recession, successful CAEs can't simply report to the audit committee or face off with management; they must shape committee members' and management's thinking by anticipating the problems, risks, and needs that lie ahead.

CAEs need the courage of their vision and convictions to steer a strategic course through the heightened risk that is testing the mettle of all organizations. The audit committee will enthusiastically embrace a CAE who exhibits sound judgment when selecting the critical issues that demand attention.

LIFE LESSON #7

Put your money where your mouth is. If you honestly believe you are right about something, then be able to demonstrate it.

---

2. TEAMWORK AND RELATIONSHIP-BUILDING SKILLS

Nothing about a job will turn you off more than having to perform under a great deal of pressure or negative energy, which is why it is important that internal auditors cultivate the trust and respect of the other professionals throughout their organization. Outstanding internal auditors invariably are good at teamwork and building strong relationships.

I'm not talking about building relationships in the C-Suite, because typically that role is reserved more for internal audit management. Instead, I'm talking about building relationships throughout the organization, in the areas, departments, functions, and activities where you do your internal audit work. Even the newest, least-experienced internal auditor has opportunities each day to build relationships.

Early in my career, as a junior member of the audit team, I would seek to establish a rapport with the individuals I was asked to interview or whose operations I was to review. I wouldn't just show up with my notepad and pen to sit there and take notes or transcribe whatever was said. I sought to interact on a person-to-person basis in the hope the person would be more open, yield better insights, and have a pleasant working experience.

Internal auditors must work hard to build relationships even before an audit engagement begins. When we know we will be returning to the same operating units throughout our tenure in internal auditing, the building of open, trusting, and enduring relationships helps ensure that each one of those engagements is going to yield more value and greater success.

Partnership with management is a phrase that some internal auditors shrink from because they worry that a "partner" can't be objective. I disagree. I think there are important ways in which we can partner with management without losing our objectivity, as long as we are not making the decisions or implementing the solutions. Obviously, decisions about where such partnering is going to occur and whether internal audit is going to support a particular business unit should emanate from the CAE in conjunction with senior management.

When I was director of Army Internal Review at the Pentagon, I was asked to be a part of a reengineering task force assembled by the Department of Defense to look at streamlining the process of reporting travel expenses. I served on that task force not as a voting member but as an adviser to the other members and to monitor the possibility that critical internal controls might be eliminated as a part of any streamlining. I find my participation in such activities to be quite valuable to my work as an auditor. And when then-Vice President Al Gore had a ceremony sometime later to present his "Hammer Awards" to various teams that had successfully reengineered key processes for the government, I went up and received my award along with the other task force members, because I was part of that partnership.

We should also be open to opportunities for teamwork within our internal audit department, not just with our clients. Internal audit is not an individual sport; it is a team effort. The same part-nering skills that internal auditors should apply while serving their audit customers can also help foster better relationships with their colleagues in internal audit. Only through intensive collaboration and teamwork, with each auditor making specialized contributions based on her or his own knowledge and experience, can we best serve our stakeholders. Even if you're a one-person staff, you need to inter-act with other senior officials as part of the enterprise management team, because those are the people you will need to work with and consult on an ongoing basis if you are going to truly add value to the operation. I can recall many instances during my career when the person in charge of a one- or two-person staff reached out to me for advice. Even though we weren't part of the same team, that person sought additional input.

As internal auditors, we need to be open to the idea that we are more effective when we are working as part of a well-coordinated team than when working alone. And it is the CAE's responsibility to ensure that everyone in internal audit appreciates the impor-tance of working together as an effective team.

3. COMMUNICATION SKILLS

An internal audit professional has to be a strong communicator. You are never too young and it is never too early in your career to begin working on your communication skills, starting with your boss if you're the CAE, with the CAE if you are a member of the internal audit staff, or with your supervisors within internal audit.

As an internal auditor, you must be able to explain to manage-ment why an engagement is being undertaken and what your role in it is going to be. If you need information during the course of the audit, you should be able to articulate why you need it, rather than simply showing up and saying, "Please give me these documents or these files." Such skills will serve you well no matter what career field you might choose later, and if you decide to stay in internal auditing, they will become increasingly important as you advance.

Internal audit executives who tend toward the stereotype of the introverted, socially awkward accountant will find it difficult, if not impossible, to build a relationship with their audit committee.

4. DIVERSITY

As a government auditor, I received regular training in matters of diversity. That training almost always focused on how to understand and work with people from different ethnic backgrounds. But diversity in the workplace is not just about differences based on race, ethnicity, gender, or other such factors. At its best, *diversity* is also about embracing a diversity of *ideas*. It's the willingness to accept people with different points of view and to hear those different points of view throughout the course of our audit work. The most successful internal auditors are always open to alternative points of view; they don't enter engagements with closed minds, and they never try to keep other people's ideas from surfacing.

As our organizations grow in complexity, we need to manage diversity in a comprehensive sense, addressing different approaches to thinking and learning. One way to encourage diversity may simply be to ensure that everyone on the internal audit staff has a "global" mindset. By thinking globally but acting locally, we can ensure that our audit recommendations are a good fit both for local management and for the organization as a whole.

In every organization where I have served as an executive, I have striven to recruit and retain a diverse team of employees while encouraging diversity of thoughts and ideas. As the CEO of the internal audit profession's worldwide body, I am constantly reminded of our cultural and ethnic diversity here in the early twenty-first century. While I believe in recruiting or promoting individuals based on their qualifications, I also believe that successful internal audit organizations should mirror the diversity of their enterprise—whether through race, gender, or other characteristics. In 2013, I was among those honored by the National Association of Black Accountants with the group's Legacy Award. I treasure it as a constant reminder that my pursuit of diversity in the profession has been recognized by others.

5. Curiosity and a Thirst for Learning

I don't think I've ever reached a point in my career where I didn't want to learn even more. When I joined the U.S. Postal Service after years of working with the Army, I wanted to know all about the core processes by which the Postal Service carried out its mission—the collection, transport, processing, and ultimate distribution of the nation's mail. The USPS handles almost 40 percent of the world's mail, and I knew I would be a more effective audit executive the more I knew about how the agency operated.

LIFE LESSON #8

Be curious and stay curious.
If you are not continuously learning new things, your
work won't be nearly as effective as it should be.

But I was like that long before my time with the Postal Service. If I was about to audit an area such as contracting and expected to undertake such audits on a regular basis, I would ask my supervisor if I could take a course in contracting. Sometimes I settled for a correspondence course because our budget didn't lend itself to regular classroom training, but I always found my supervisors open to the idea of continuing education when I found cost-effective ways of getting it.

Continuous learning is more than a matter of taking a new training course each year. Internal auditors must maintain a sense of curiosity throughout their careers. Some learning is best accomplished through formal training and development programs or the pursuit of a professional certification. But some of the most important lessons for internal auditors can emerge from rotational assignments, unusual projects, or self-guided learning. Our passion for new and useful information can prove vital when assessing risk, interviewing clients, or undertaking any other phase of our audit work. Some learning results from well-placed questions during an audit; other times it's simply the result of a voracious appetite for reading.

The average internal auditor receives roughly forty to eighty hours of formal training each year, which is not sufficient if you aspire to become a world-class internal auditor. Leading internal audit departments are starting to expect much more, even from their most experienced staff. For example, internal auditors at Raytheon International receive 200 hours of internal training annually and generally match that on their own time by studying for the certified internal auditor (CIA) or other professional designations.

Most organizations don't yet require that level of formal training, but internal auditors with a true passion for excellence are always looking for opportunities to expand their knowledge, regardless of audit schedules, fiscal budgets, or workplace logistics. These days we are fortunate to have an almost unlimited variety of seminars, conferences, college courses, online training sessions, workshops, publications, chapter meetings, and roundtable events for internal auditors. Keeping our auditing skills fresh has never been easier.

Still, making the most of our learning opportunities can require tremendous dedication. It's not enough to be a continuous learner; we must also ensure we are learning the *right things*. Too many internal auditors concentrate on a narrow range of specialized knowledge, but to advance into internal audit management requires a deep understanding of a wide range of business and industry practices. The further you progress in your career, the more important the non-technical skills can become. If all you have done is lead information security audits or financial audits, for example, then you may not have a good grasp of the risks and controls in areas such as operations and compliance.

Regardless of their specialties, world-class internal auditors must have exceptional technical skills, a strong grasp of risks and controls, and a deep understanding of how the risks affect the bottom line. Professional certifications such as the CIA or CPA can demonstrate that you have this understanding, but more and more senior leaders are looking for a kind of broad experience that supplements and enhances those certificates.

Your career is in *your* hands—it's up to *you* to make the most of it. Most of us truly enjoy opportunities for continuing education. But if you are one of the few who do not, just remember the words of Muhammad Ali: "I hated every minute of training, but I said, 'Don't quit. Suffer now and live the rest of your life as a champion.'"

LIFE LESSON #9

You make your own breaks. If you are not willing to try anything new, success may pass you by.

I learned this life lesson the hard way, back in the late 1970s when I was just beginning my career in FORSCOM Internal Review. My supervisor, Bernie Shell, came to me one day and said, "You know, there is this new certified internal auditor designation that The Institute of Internal Auditors is beginning to offer to people who have two years of experience. All you have to do to get the CIA certification is to verify your two years of experience, pay the fee, and you get certified."

This was when The IIA first began offering the CIA designation. I looked over the material that Bernie gave me and said, "Why would I ever want that? I've never even heard of it, and that's a lot of money (I think the fee was $100 at the time). I'm not going to do it."

Boy, was I wrong! Today, the CIA designation is one of the most respected certifications in the world. I remembered my foolish mistake fifteen years later as I sat in my home office late at night in Washington, studying to take the exam for CIA certification. I had missed that earlier opportunity to obtain the designation without the test, but now I retell that story to people around the world and say, "Don't miss your opportunity to get your certification." Besides,

I'm actually better off, because I had to resume studying so I could pass the test.

Essential Characteristics of a Modern CAE

Once upon a time, the path to becoming a CAE was a fairly clear-cut proposition. You obtained an accounting degree and a professional certification, then you waited.

Today, the rules are different. If you expect your technical knowledge to lead to that job as a CAE, you might have a long wait. It's estimated that within Fortune 500 companies, almost half of all new CAEs these days are recruited from outside internal auditing altogether.

In my experience, the best CAEs are generally career internal audit professionals. All of the attributes discussed earlier in this chapter will continue to be important as you progress up the career ladder to becoming a CAE. But there are also a number of talented CAEs who don't come with that background. If I look at successful CAEs—regardless of their background—there are a handful of characteristics that the very best all have in common.

A characteristic that most outstanding CAEs possess is superior business acumen. They know how to run their department effectively, because if you can't run internal audit effectively, and others in the business know it, it undermines your credibility when you are trying to advise them on the sound business practices that they should undertake.

While recent internal audit surveys indicate that business acumen qualifies as a crucial attribute for internal audit professionals to possess, conversations with leaders in the profession indicate that this general attribute area consists of numerous equally important dimensions, including:

- Natural inquisitiveness

- Persuasiveness

- Change-management proficiency

- Service orientation

- Ability to recognize and respond to diverse thinking, learning, and cultural mindsets

- Global mindset

From my experience, highly effective CAEs view their internal audit function as a business unit and consider the rest of the organization's population as their unit's customer base. The goal then is to drive higher *sales* (or demand for internal audit support) by increasing customer satisfaction and demonstrating the value that internal audit brings to the table. Backed by a strong business outlook, internal audit is no longer viewed as an unavoidable irritant but as a business partner that can help save money, eliminate weak practices, improve efficiency, and ameliorate risk.

CAEs must also be able to develop and cultivate the talent around them. They need to help produce future internal audit leaders and the future leaders of their own companies and organizations. That means investing in, understanding, and taking an interest in their most important resource—their people. If they do not appreciate and recognize their team's contributions, they are not realizing their full potential as leaders and are unlikely to succeed.

LIFE LESSON #10

Retaining the best internal audit talent requires a continuous effort on the part of the CAE and the unit's other managers and staff.

Any success I enjoyed during my career as an audit executive was first and foremost the result of the executive talent that surrounded me. Whether it was Bob Shaw at FORSCOM, Bill O'Hare and Bob Barnhart at the Pentagon, Colleen McAntee and

Bob Emmons at the Postal Service OIG, or Ben Wagner at TVA, I would have struggled enormously without them.

Such extraordinary professionals, and the scores of others who support us, account for the success we achieve when we meet or exceed the expectations of our stakeholders.

Additional Critical Characteristics

In this chapter, I have walked you through what I consider to be the characteristics critical to the success of an internal auditor and a CAE. But there are other personal qualities that all audit professionals should possess. I'd like to round out the chapter with some of these necessary characteristics.

1. OBJECTIVITY

Objectivity is an unbiased mental attitude that allows internal auditors to perform engagements in such a manner that they believe in the work product and accept no compromises in the product's quality. Objectivity requires that internal auditors do not subordinate their judgment on audit matters to others.[1]

I remember a conversation I had with an Army internal review chief at one of our subordinate commands who was trying to get me involved in helping him and his organization. He said, "My commander won't let me be independent."

I said, "But you are not supposed to be independent of your commander (CEO). You are not independent. You should be objective." There is no such thing as a totally independent auditor; we all have dependencies. The president of the United States is dependent on votes to gain and retain the office. I'm dependent on my board of directors. I'm frustrated by people who confuse independence with objectivity.

Objectivity is the process that allows an internal auditor to make impartial, unbiased judgments. Often people confuse the organizational attribute of *independence* with the individual attribute of *objectivity*, which internal auditors are expected to maintain. Independence is an organizational attribute; it is freedom from the conditions that can threaten the ability of an internal audit activity or a CAE to carry out their responsibilities in an unbiased manner.

As internal audit professionals, we may not be independent of the organization, yet we must maintain our objectivity when conducting our work within the organization. The internal audit activity should be independent, and the internal audit professionals behind it should remain objective. I will come back to this later in the book.

2. PASSION

It is virtually impossible to be very good at something you don't really like to do. Successful internal auditors have a deep interest in, and intense enthusiasm for, their work. Some are more passionate about it than others, but long-term success cannot be sustained without this passion.

3. WORK ETHIC

One thing my father passed on to me was a strong work ethic. For me, success in business requires that I consistently meet the quality, cost, and timing expectations of my *stakeholders/ customers*. And such success does not come without hard work. Successful internal auditors must not only work hard, they must also work smart. They get the right things done the right way at the right time.

4. CURIOSITY

A natural curiosity and desire to dig deeper is a good trait for an internal auditor, for sometimes the information needed to judge something may not always be obvious. Successful internal auditors learn that they may need to ask more probing questions to gain the necessary understanding of how things work and why they work the way they do.

5. CREATIVITY

Most internal auditors like to solve problems. However, sometimes the solutions to many problems are not always obvious. Successful internal auditors must be creative and think outside the box to generate the kinds of ideas valued by management and other stakeholders.

6. INITIATIVE

Successful internal auditors are self-starters. They voluntarily seek out and pursue opportunities to add value to their organizations and want to play the role of change agent within them.

7. FLEXIBILITY

Change is the only constant in today's business world. Successful organizations continuously adapt to change, even as that change brings with it new risks that must be managed. Successful internal auditors embrace change; they adapt quickly to new situations and challenges.

The characteristics described above illustrate the inherent personal qualities that are required to succeed as an internal auditor. Does this mean that someone lacking one or more of these traits is destined to fail as an internal auditor? Not necessarily. These qualities can be exercised—and can be strengthened if desired.[2]

The core characteristics I have outlined in this chapter are essential to your success in the internal audit profession. Yet, they're also an essential part of building relationships with stakeholders, because without stakeholders, there is no mission.

Leveraging Our Strengths

It is critical that CAEs and internal auditors pursue continuous excellence and exemplify the core characteristics outlined in this chapter. Developing each of these attributes must be a key priority for each member of our profession, but developing them is a process that takes time and patience.

Regardless of how rapidly we develop these characteristics, there are two critical factors we must never forget. First, we must augment these core characteristics with the expertise needed to address the key risks our organizations face. Second, we must ensure that the characteristics and critical skills we develop are aligned with the needs and expectations of our key stakeholders—whose importance we will explore in much greater detail in chapter 3.

CHAPTER 3

No Stakeholders? No Mission

Early in my career, I took for granted that internal auditing existed simply because it was necessary. Very rarely did anyone use terms like *customers* or *stakeholders;* I don't remember ever hearing those terms during my first decade in the business. I knew that U.S. Army regulations at the time required that every activity have an internal review function, so I assumed we were there simply because we had to be. Resources were plentiful, and no one was really scrutinizing the value that we delivered, which isn't surprising. People generally don't begin to question the value of something until it becomes difficult to pay for it.

That all changed for those of us in the military by the end of the 1980s. The Berlin Wall came down, the Cold War ended, and the U.S. Department of Defense—for the first time in more than five decades—faced the prospect of significantly downsizing as other government programs began clamoring for a piece of what was called the *peace dividend.*[1]

Military budgets started shrinking dramatically. Leaders in the Army and throughout the Defense Department began to scrutinize the value they were receiving for the money they were spending on internal auditing. Resources in my area, Army Internal Review, were in free fall. More than 400 positions were eliminated from various internal review departments around the world in just three years.

When I moved to the Pentagon as the Army's Director of Internal Review in the fall of 1993, one of my first conversations was with Neil Ginnetti, Principal Deputy Assistant Secretary of the Army at the time and a gentleman for whom I grew to have a great deal of respect. He sat down with me that first week on the job to remind me of the dramatic reductions underway in internal review.

"As you know, Richard, the Army's Internal Review resources are being decimated," he said. In just five years, Internal Review's head count worldwide had been slashed from 2,100 to 1,400. "I need you to figure out how to put a stop to it!" Ginnetti told me.

I responded by saying, "I agree with you, Neil. It's a big concern. But before I can help figure out *how to stop it*, I have to understand *why it's happening*." The Army overall wasn't shrinking that fast. And in some internal review offices, resources were down 75 percent in less than four years.

So I set off on a six-week tour of internal review operations, with stops at about twenty-four offices, including sites in Japan, Hawaii, and all over the United States. At each location, I would sit down with the commander, the chief of staff, or the controller; by regulation, internal review had to report to the commander or chief of staff. In most cases, those I interviewed would tell me, "I like the internal review team. They are nice guys, and they do good work."

"But why did you downsize them?" I would ask. "Why did you cut internal review by 75 percent last year, when you had only about a 10 percent cut in your overall budget?"

Their responses were eye-opening. "You know, those guys come in and tell me what I already know," some of them said. Others responded, "They tell me things are broken, but I already know they are broken. *I need somebody who can tell me how to fix them*." Conversely, more than once I heard, "Sometimes I only need to know 'what time it is,' but the internal review guys insist on giving me voluminous reports that tell me 'how to build the watch.'"

LIFE LESSON #11

*If stakeholders don't value your internal audits,
eventually they won't value internal auditors, either.*

In preparing for this book, I reviewed some of my notes from that period, and concluded that the sharp reductions in internal review were occurring for three reasons:

1. The Army was downsizing and cutting back drastically on spending throughout its operations.

2. Our products and services were not what they should have been.

3. Our performance wasn't what it should have been.

Downsizing

There was really nothing we could do about the Army's down-sizing. That was a macro issue of strategic significance far bigger than what any of us in internal review could hope to influence. It was the current reality, and one would naturally expect that, if the organization we served was getting smaller, we would need to get smaller, too.

Products and Services

There were clearly some things we could do about our products and our services. I was being told that the full-scope audits that we historically had performed—evaluating an entire department or system or activity—were not really what our stakeholders wanted. They considered them laborious, cumbersome, and time-consuming.

I also traced some of our difficulties to rigid planning cycles and inflexible policies that dictated what had to be documented in our reports and work papers, and when.

I discovered that our audit reports were often considered by stakeholders to be too focused on compliance issues and not focused enough on ways to help them improve the efficiency and effectiveness of their operations.

Finally, I noted that a lot of our audits were irrelevant. It's not that they lacked all merit, but they weren't focusing on the biggest risks then facing the Army—they didn't relate to the key issues being discussed and debated throughout the organization. Of course, few internal auditors anywhere were talking a lot about risk-based auditing in 1993, and the Army was no different. In military terms, we in internal review hadn't learned how to *pick our battles*, so we were missing out on some of our biggest opportunities to add value to our organization.

Weak Performance

As I looked back at my notes, I realized our performance was considered weak because our stakeholders viewed us as not being *mission-oriented*. Our commanders had a mission: to ensure our armed forces were trained, equipped, and ready for deployment when needed for our national defense. But internal review didn't necessarily view our commands' missions as the ones we needed to focus on as auditors.

I also heard complaints that we were not very *customer-oriented*. Excessive overhead had become a problem, and the quality of our work had suffered. I noted that some internal review offices had been downsized in such a way that they were top-heavy with management and administration. I remember a department that at one time had five staff—a chief or director, a secretary, and three audit staff. Two positions were eliminated—a 40 percent reduction—but the cuts had been allowed to occur through attrition, so when two of the three audit staffers departed, the department was left with one chief, one secretary, and one auditor. In effect, the department had absorbed a 66 percent reduction in internal audit capability, rather than 40 percent.

One commander noted that he had spent almost $1 million on the department the previous year, yet had received only five reports. Although the number of reports really shouldn't be used to determine the value received, clearly in his mind there was a correlation.

"Look, they are good guys and ladies," more than one commander said of their internal review staff during my six-week tour. "I really appreciate what they do, and they are professionals. But at the end of the day, if I've got to take a cut in spending, and I have to choose between [keeping] the internal audit function and support for family housing for soldiers, I'm going to choose the family housing, and we are going to cut down on our audit capability."

Such comments were particularly unfortunate because I considered that a false dilemma; if we had truly been effective as internal auditors, we would have addressed the problem and identified sufficient savings, allowing a commander to fund both the internal review office and the family housing budgets.

Somehow, I had to convince these commanders that we were all in this together and needed to work as a team. I formed a steering group comprising the chiefs of internal review from all the major Army commands. The resulting strategic plan for Army Internal Review included five key steps:

1. Defining our customers and their needs.

2. Defining our mission.

3. Articulating assumptions and our values.

4. Forging an internal review vision, goals, and supporting actions.

5. Assessing our progress.

Our strategy worked. Army-wide, internal review's return on investment (the cost of operations versus identified, agreed-to savings) jumped from 3-to-1 in 1992 to an astounding 24-to-1 by 1996. The number of audit engagements completed worldwide doubled over the same period, from about 2,200 in 1993 to more than 4,400 in 1996. Although downsizing continued throughout the Army, internal review no longer shrank at a disproportionate rate.

That was the first time I realized that internal auditors have stakeholders, and that disenchanted stakeholders are hazardous to an internal audit operation's health. In the years since then, I have seen similar problems crop up in the corporate sector; while not as widespread as in the military, in some instances, the stakeholders' dissatisfaction with a corporate internal audit function led to the operation's complete outsourcing—or worse yet, its abolishment.

Who Are Our Stakeholders?

A stakeholder is any party with a direct or indirect interest in an organization's activities and outcomes. Internal auditors typically have several groups of stakeholders within a company or an organization, all of whose needs should be considered.

I. PRIMARY STAKEHOLDERS

Identifying your primary stakeholders is the most important step. I generally consider primary stakeholders to include:

- The organization's audit committee and board (and elected officials in the case of government agencies).

- The CEO or overall head of the enterprise.

- The chief financial officer (CFO) or the individual to whom the CAE reports administratively.

- The other chief officers of the enterprise (in some cases).

When we speak about internal audit stakeholders in the twenty-first century, it's often in terms of the various groups with an interest in the operation. The most important group for an internal audit department in the corporate setting is the board of directors. The board has critical oversight responsibilities, and its members are the pinnacle of governance within the corporation.

A board, through its audit committee, is generally looking to internal audit for assurance. Its members want to know, and they want internal audit to assure them, that the corporation's various risks are being appropriately managed through well-designed and well-administered internal controls.

Audit committee members often talk about wanting "no surprises." When you consider the size and complexity of some organizations, avoiding surprises is a tall order. Boards don't want internal auditors merely looking in the rearview mirror; they want us to be their eyes and ears in the here and now. Internal audit historically has largely been about hindsight, but today's stakeholders want insight as well.

Top managers also look to internal audit for assurance and insight, though they often would prefer we not be so quick to share with the board. Management is also seeking "value for money" from internal audit. Much like those Army commanders who bent my ear twenty years ago, today's corporate executives are always weighing their investment in internal audit against its perceived value. My first piece of advice to a new CAE is "assess these stakeholders' needs and expectations and don't overlook the 'value proposition.'"

2. Secondary Stakeholders

Internal audit's secondary stakeholders include business-unit executives and other leaders not identified as primary stakeholders. These executives are the ones who typically head up the business units and operations on which our audits are focused. They are what we used to call *auditees*; in the twenty-first century, we need to think of them as *clients*. We should try to focus our work in such a way that it not only addresses the needs of our primary stakeholders but also adds value for these business-unit executives. Much like the Army commanders I dealt with in the early 1990s, these executives often already know they have problems—they are looking for solutions. They need our help designing and implementing effective internal controls.

They also view us as business partners. They would like us to focus more on areas they consider high risk or of particular significance to them. They, too, are looking for insight, and increasingly they consider us a source of talent for their business units.

3. TERTIARY STAKEHOLDERS

Internal audit's other stakeholders may include:

- Employees (and, in some cases, retirees) of the enterprise.

- Investment analysts and others with an interest in the performance of the enterprise and the effectiveness of risk management and internal controls.

- Shareholders.

- External auditors and regulators.

- The general public (including news media for government auditors).

Regulators are an increasingly important stakeholder group. They are very interested in making sure internal auditors are independent and can provide assurance on risks and controls. They are seeking assurance that the organization is in compliance with government laws, regulations, and policies and is not likely to fall victim to a significant scandal or calamity.

Internal audit's stakeholders and their expectations can vary dramatically from one organization to the next. Every CAE must continuously review current and potential stakeholder groups and reassess their needs and expectations. It is important to recognize that their needs and expectations are not static—they can change dramatically in a short period of time. In the mid-2000s, for example, corporate internal audit stakeholders were mainly seeking assurance on the adequacy of internal controls over financial reporting because of the newly enacted Sarbanes-Oxley legislation. By the end of the decade, however, expectations had shifted within many companies, and their internal auditors were looked to for assurance on the adequacy of the operation's risk management and internal controls, and insight into cost-reduction and cost-containment opportunities.

CAEs will from time to time encounter conflicts between the expectations of different stakeholders. In such situations, I always advise the CAEs to prioritize their activities and, if necessary, discuss apparent conflicts with the stakeholders involved. Nothing can be more frustrating for a CAE than having an audit committee with a set of expectations that differs dramatically from those of the CEO. Having an open and honest discussion with the parties to reconcile the differences will go a long way toward ensuring internal audit's ultimate success.

Education is another way to influence stakeholder expectations. For instance, CAEs can educate management and the audit committee on what internal audit really does or can do—helping set realistic expectations up front and addressing any confusion. Marketing also can help CAEs educate stakeholders on the important role internal auditors play within the organization.

Stakeholder Concerns About Internal Audit

What sorts of things are stakeholders concerned about? Here are some of the things I hear often during one-on-one conversations with some of internal auditing's key stakeholders.

Executive Management

Management frequently laments that internal audit doesn't have an adequate knowledge of "the business."

You can't really have a strong and effective internal audit function, they say, if you don't have a good grasp of what the organization does or of the issues and risks—including strategic business risks—faced not only of your company but of the industry in which it operates.

Management is concerned that we are not very efficient or innovative. I am going to talk about innovation in a later chapter, but the concern about efficiency may be management's way of signaling that it doesn't get as much out of internal audit as it should. Again, these are some of the same basic concerns that various stakeholders were sharing with me two decades ago.

Management is looking for insight, advice, and assistance, but often we just want to offer assurance. They also see at least the possibility that we duplicate other risk management, compliance, and oversight functions within the organization. They may see us undertaking risk assessments at the same time and in the same manner as the chief risk officer (CRO). They may see us conducting investigations that others also have the power to undertake. So they are concerned about overlap. In such instances, we need to coordinate closely with those other lines of defense so we don't overlap—or, if we do, we can explain why. We also must be sensitive to what I refer to as "audit fatigue."

Audit Committees

When I spoke recently to a group of audit committee members and board members, generally one of their biggest concerns about internal audit was communication.

They said internal auditors are not great communicators when it comes to interacting with their audit committee and the full board of directors. I hear this often.

Sure, we may issue forty audit reports a year, but we never step back and say how well we think the enterprise or business unit is controlled overall. I'll cover communications in a later chapter, but suffice it to say that this is an area upon which many CAEs need to focus.

Stakeholders increasingly want us to provide assurance on the effectiveness of strategic risk management, which some internal auditors are reluctant to do because we're not quite sure how to go about it. It's very easy to audit the effectiveness of internal controls; it's a lot more difficult to provide assurance related to key business strategies and key business risks.

Finally, stakeholders are looking for insight.

Maybe your stakeholders are not concerned about these issues, but other underlying issues can also erode support. Regardless of the cause, here are some key indicators that a serious expectations gap is forming between an internal audit unit and its stakeholders.

Five Signs That Stakeholder Support Is Waning

When CAEs and their staff are not meeting stakeholder expectations, warning signs typically appear, indicating that the support they once enjoyed is starting to erode.

1. LACKLUSTER RESPONSE TO THE RISK ASSESSMENTS.

If you're having trouble getting stakeholders to respond during the annual risk assessment, that's a problem. Virtually all executives and board members have things that keep them awake at night, so if they aren't sharing their concerns with you, it could mean they don't trust you to act on them or don't think your team has the ability to address them.

As an internal auditor, you go through this process at least annually (though I hope much more often). If your stakeholders don't appear interested in the risk assessment, offering you little or no food for thought, that's not a good sign.

It may mean they view your risk assessment as irrelevant; perhaps they have gone through the process with you before but concluded that nothing had come of it.

2. THE PHONE NEVER RINGS.

Yes, this is a throwback to an earlier time, not that long ago, when we used phones a lot more than we do now. Email or instant messaging may be your main form of business communication these days. Regardless of method used, if no one is reaching out to internal audit to ask that you address an emerging risk or evaluate a developing situation, it's likely your stakeholders don't see you as responsive or a resource.

Delivering value is the key to long-term success for any internal audit operation. If top executives and business unit leaders don't think internal audit adds value to the organization, they won't seek you out when a problem arises.

3. Breakaway republics.

When business units start creating their own audit teams (or elements within a unit that duplicate the capabilities of internal audit), chances are you're not living up to their expectations.

When different business groups within an organization come to the conclusion that internal audit isn't serving their needs, they may start to set up review functions of their own. They may not call them internal audit, but they do the same kind of work. That's a sign those stakeholders don't see the value of internal audit or don't think it can be trusted.

4. Reduced resources.

There are times when financial pressures mandate cutbacks throughout a company. When resources are reduced across an organization, it's only natural to expect reductions in internal audit's resources, too. But if your unit's budget is slashed disproportionately compared with other departments, as was the situation with the Army's Internal Review offices in the 1990s, that's a clear indicator that your stakeholders don't see enough value in your work. Companies invest in what they value, and if their investment in internal audit is shrinking when overall budgets are stable or expanding, it's a sign that an expectations gap may have developed.

5. THE EXTERNAL QUALITY ASSESSMENT IS NOT YOUR IDEA.

IIA Standard 1312: External Assessments requires external quality assessments of internal audit departments at least once every five years. The internal audit department should always be the one proactively pushing for that assessment; if your stakeholders independently initiate a quality assessment, it is likely they have concerns about your department and are looking for validation.

If you haven't had an external quality assessment for a few years, and you get a call from the CEO, the CFO, or even the audit committee, and they say, "We'd like you to get a quality assessment"—or, worse yet, they take the lead in identifying who is going to come and do the assessment—that may be the clearest sign possible that something is seriously wrong between your unit and its stakeholders.

Can We Improve Stakeholders' Support?

What can internal audit do to improve stakeholder support? It starts with how internal audit interacts and communicates with management. Strong stakeholder-auditor relationships are always underpinned by clear communication, trust, and respect. In such cases, the stakeholders will see internal audit as a valuable resource; will respect the CAE; and will look to internal audit for insight, hindsight, and, yes, sometimes even foresight, which I discuss in the concluding chapter of this book.

CAEs strive to add value and be viewed as leading a high-performing internal audit function.

Meeting or, better yet, exceeding their stakeholders' specific expectations is essential in demonstrating the value internal auditors bring to the organization. To do that, it is also essential that CAEs understand how stakeholders determine whether their expectations are being met and, therefore, whether internal audit's efforts are viewed as "value-added" activities.

During the only real hiatus I took from internal auditing in my career, I spent some time as an operations research analyst in the U.S. Army Forces Command's Programming and Cost Analysis Division. There I learned the importance of assessing and meeting stakeholders' expectations regardless of the role one plays in an organization.

Back then, in 1985, the Army was just beginning to experiment with third-party contracting. One project in which I became deeply involved was the testing of third-party contracting for child-care centers. Fort Lewis, located southwest of Tacoma in Washington state, was chosen as the site for this experiment. Under the direction of Congress, the Army was charged with evaluating whether an outside party could design, construct, and operate a child-care center for the offspring of soldiers and other staff as efficiently and effectively as the Army, which historically had operated such centers itself.

A project this important and complex had many stakeholders. Not only were the military officials responsible for the quality of child-care services keenly interested in the outcome, other important stakeholders included Congress, the child-care industry, and, most importantly (from my perspective), the soldiers and spouses whose children would be entrusted to whichever operating model was ultimately adopted. Even though I was only a GS13 cost analyst, I was given a very important role in the evaluation process, and I took my stakeholder responsibilities quite seriously.

At the start of the project, the Army's child-care professionals were strongly opposed to letting someone other than the Army operate these facilities. They suggested, among other things, that the third-party providers would be much more expensive. I was appointed to lead the development of an objective evaluation methodology by which various commercial vendors' proposals could be evaluated and compared with an Army proposal.

I worked on this project for many months, including several weeks spent at Fort Lewis, where we evaluated the vendors' complex proposals and compared them with the Army's plan from the standpoint of costs and other factors. The implications were huge, because if a non-Army business could win this competition, these third-party contractors could potentially take over operation of child-care centers worldwide—not just for the U.S. Army but for the Navy and Air Force as well.

For me, it was a great opportunity and a great experience. As it turned out, the third-party contracts were far less costly than the Army-run proposal and offered other advantages as well. As a result, virtually all child-care centers on Army installations today are run by third-party vendors. And it was clearly a value-added activity for the Army's stakeholders.

LIFE LESSON #12

Know your stakeholders and strive continuously to meet or exceed their expectations.

Just as important as identifying your stakeholders' expectations is keeping an eye out for any changes in those expectations over time. For example, many stakeholders are now raising their expectations for internal audit in terms of its handling of risk and risk management, just as they did following passage of Sarbanes-Oxley. It is essential that CAEs solicit stakeholder feedback in an ongoing, systematic manner and update their internal audit strategies and plans as needed to address any changes. More specifically, CAEs need to continually develop processes for understanding stakeholders' expectations and perceptions, finding ways to meet those expectations, measuring and reporting results relative to those expectations, and periodically reassessing expectations.

Assessing and addressing stakeholder expectations must be a proactive process, not a passive activity. In my experience, stakeholders typically don't approach the CAE to initiate a discussion unless an expectations gap has already formed. By then, the damage is already done.

I strongly urge CAEs to actively engage in stakeholder expectation assessments as an ongoing part of their operations. In a recent IIA Audit Executive Center survey, respondents were asked which strategies they deployed to assess stakeholder expectations. The results were eye-opening:

1. Ongoing informal discussions with audit committee chair to assess expectations—69 percent.

2. Regular formal meetings with key stakeholders to assess expectations—59 percent.

3. Discussions with full audit committee to assess collective expectations—57 percent.

4. Formal surveys of stakeholders to assess expectations/performance—40 percent.

5. Discussions with the full executive leadership/management team in the same room to assess collective expectations/performance—26 percent.[2]

If it is true that 30 percent of CAEs do not talk informally with their audit committee chairman about stakeholder expectations, then I fear a key segment of our profession is missing out on a key opportunity. In my experience, the most meaningful feedback on expectations comes from such informal conversations—not from structured meetings or surveys.

Meeting Expectations and Maintaining Alignment

If you sense an expectations gap exists, the obvious question is what can I do to close it? I think the best way to start is to acknowledge the elephant in the room and simply say, "I understand that we may not be meeting your needs and expectations, and we are recommitting ourselves to doing a better job."

Seek clarity. Get honest feedback on your strengths and weaknesses. Enlist the help of your stakeholders to make your internal audit operation more effective. It's not enough to simply declare that you are going to do better; you need to engage your stakeholders in the process.

The rehabilitation process can be difficult, but recognizing that you have a problem is half the battle.

The entire process constitutes a *life cycle* for aligning, maintaining, and meeting expectations that is a necessary part of the internal audit department's ongoing operations. This "stakeholder expectation life cycle" consists of four key components:

UNDERSTANDING THE CURRENT EXPECTATIONS OF KEY STAKEHOLDERS

Through ongoing discussions, CAEs can identify the specific expectations of their key stakeholders and articulate them in a short list of specific actions that stakeholders think add value to the organization. Having a clear understanding of what is important to them—what is *on their mind*—is critical. To accomplish this, it's imperative for CAEs to invest the necessary time and resources in understanding the key challenges, issues, and opportunities that are relevant to these stakeholders.

Once it's created, the list needs to be validated with the key stakeholders to ensure their support. It should also be communicated to other stakeholders and to internal audit personnel. Finally, the CAE should ensure that the internal audit charter reflects the specific expectations of the key stakeholders. Fully understanding their view of the organization's challenges, issues, and opportunities is essential for the long-term success of any internal audit department.

Building and Maintaining the Capabilities to Deliver on the Expectations

Delivering on stakeholders' expectations is paramount to the success of the internal audit function. To do so, CAEs need to perform a robust gap assessment that matches internal audit's current capabilities and skills to each expectation. CAEs should then draft or update a strategic plan that builds or enhances internal audit's capabilities so they can meet those expectations. CAEs also can use expectations as filters to identify the best practices for meeting stakeholders' needs.

Creating a Process to Measure and Report on the Achievement of Specific Expectations

A stakeholder management strategy can be a powerful means of assimilating the many insights gained by members of your internal audit team from the multitude of planned and unplanned interactions with key stakeholders. This big-picture approach should provide a collective, integrated view of all stakeholders. With such a strategy, tactics for interacting with each stakeholder can be developed.

Three main activities CAEs can undertake to measure the efficiency and effectiveness of internal audit's efforts to meet stakeholder expectations: developing and using a balanced scorecard, creating appropriate measures to gauge performance, and developing appropriate objectives and periodic reporting mechanisms. CAEs should view this as their opportunity to demonstrate specifically and tangibly how they performed relative to their stakeholder expectations and added-value goals.

Establishing Processes to Reassess Stakeholder Expectations Periodically

Finally, CAEs need to establish a time frame and a process for reassessing stakeholders' expectations at least annually. CAEs should identify events, such as the addition of new audit committee members, that would trigger such reassessments. Because communication is key to understanding stakeholder expectations and raising those expectations to the next level, it is important for CAEs to communicate with stakeholders throughout the year as opportunities and issues arise and to deliver what they said they were going to deliver.

One of the most pivotal aspects of a stakeholder management strategy is setting up the right communication protocol for each target audience. Formal protocols for communication encourage the exchange of information with stakeholders and help CAEs during audit planning and execution.

Ensuring Continued Alignment

Once CAEs have identified their stakeholders, those stakeholders' expectations, and ways to meet those expectations, they need to ensure that their internal audit efforts consistently and continually address the stakeholders' key concerns. Although stakeholder expectations do not typically change dramatically from year to year, when they do change, the shift can often take internal auditors by surprise.

CAEs should watch for events that may trigger a change in stakeholder expectations. For example, a new audit committee chair, CEO, or even CFO can signal a shift in stakeholder expectations as new people often bring new views with them. Also, outside influences such as new compliance requirements or the current renewed focus on risk management may cause many stakeholders to shift expectations regarding internal audit's involvement and coverage. Finally, internal events, including changes in business strategy, may alter stakeholder expectations pertaining to the focus of internal audit's work.

The internal audit departments that have the most noticeable stature with executive management are those whose CAEs and staff understand their stakeholders and never forget that stakeholder expectations are a moving target. The audit departments that were successful at one time but later failed often failed to act when their stakeholders' expectations changed.

If we continuously realign the delivery of our services to meet the evolving expectations of our stakeholders, we are more likely to deliver the value they are seeking.

CHAPTER 4

The Importance of Value

I once had the opportunity to lead an external quality assessment for the internal audit department of a large U.S. health-care provider. As I interviewed the company's key executives and board members, one word came up over and over: *value.*

The CEO noted that internal audit provided *extraordinary value* for the company as a "trusted source of assurance on compliance, risk management, and internal controls." The CFO said internal audit provided *value* by ensuring the effectiveness of the business' financial controls. Other executives saw the *value* in the internal audit department's annual enterprise risk assessment, which many said they used as a road map for managing risks within the company. And, according to the chairman of the company's audit committee, board members saw *value* in internal audit because it enabled them to "sleep better" knowing that such "a strong and effective oversight function was keeping a watchful eye on risks, controls, and compliance in the company."

From my experience in leading external quality assessments, use of the word *value* by internal audit stakeholders is not uncommon. What made the interviews with the health-care executives noteworthy was the extraordinary degree to which the stakeholders appreciated the value they received from the company's internal audits. As I discovered during the course of the assessment, this was no accident. Delivering value to stakeholders was part of that internal audit department's culture, from the CAE down to the least-senior member of the one hundred-person staff.

That experience also reinforced a lesson that I had learned early in my career—delivering value is an overarching imperative for internal auditors.

The Essence of Value for Internal Auditing

I sometimes think *value* is the least appreciated word in The IIA's definition of internal auditing. If an internal audit department does not add value to the organization it serves, then it really isn't fulfilling its reason for being. Every element of an organization should be adding value to the operation, and internal audit is no different. When internal audit fails to generate value for the organization, then it is simply another cost center—a drain on company resources.

The question then is, "Where is the value?" The answer, as I have preached for many years, is, "In the eye of the beholder." We can't fairly define our value to others, though I've seen it done many times. Internal auditors who try to define the value of their function will often say, "We measure it by the number of reports we issue. We measure it by the number of individuals in our department who have their certification. We measure it by the number of recommendations in our reports." But our stakeholders aren't likely to cite those measurements in assessing our value. And the value of internal audit has to be defined by its stakeholders.

"We don't think you are of any value to us because you have yet to help us fix a problem we're having," management might say. "Besides, we don't get any value from internal audit because you cost us more money than you save us."

Ultimately, it is for others to decide whether we are valuable or not. If they say we aren't, the problem may be that we simply aren't adding enough value to the operation—or it may be that we haven't helped our stakeholders to appreciate the value we add. Either way, we must address the problem.

The Value Proposition

Back in 2008, The IIA formed a task force under the leadership of former IIA Chairman Denny Beran. Its mission: explore stakeholders' expectations and determine what it is that internal auditors should deliver in the way of value. By 2010, the task force submitted its report and recommendations to The IIA's Board of Directors. The "value proposition" illustration below sums up its work.

INTERNAL AUDITING = ASSURANCE, INSIGHT AND OBJECTIVITY[1]

ASSURANCE

INTERNAL AUDITING

INSIGHT   OBJECTIVITY

The task force's value proposition for internal audit rests on three core concepts: assurance, insight, and objectivity. Internal auditors ignore them at their own risk.

I learned this lesson during the early part of my career in Internal Review at U.S. Army Forces Command (FORSCOM), after I had completed a quality assessment of one of the command's biggest internal review offices.

As with all of our quality assurance reviews, I undertook a comprehensive assessment of the department, evaluated its conformance with applicable standards, and had extensive discussions with the CAE. I came away thinking this might be one of the best internal review departments I had ever seen. It was led by a bright CAE who appeared to have a firm grasp on the department's role. The team's work was impeccable and in accordance with the Yellow Book (Government Accountability Office Government Audit Standards). I gave them high marks.

So imagine my surprise less than two years later when I learned that very same internal review office had been abolished and the CAE reassigned to another area.

LIFE LESSON #13

Your key stakeholders have the last word on whether you are doing your job well. And they judge an internal audit function not by how well-run it is, but by the value it generates for them.

I couldn't believe it. I even thought the department might have fallen victim to a conspiracy of some sort—its work had been that good. But as I asked around to find out what had happened, I learned that the commander, the chief of staff, and the controller had concluded they weren't getting any value from their internal review office—at a time when the downsizing of the Army was underway—and one more internal review casualty had just been claimed.

To help internal auditors understand the value proposition's three core elements, each element can be further defined:

1. *Assurance* = **Governance, Risk, and Control:** Internal auditing provides assurance on the organization's governance, risk management, and control processes to help the organization achieve its strategic, operational, financial, and compliance objectives.

2. *Insight* = **Catalyst, Analyses, and Assessments:** Internal auditing is a catalyst for improving an organization's effectiveness and efficiency by providing insight and recommendations based on analyses and assessments of data and business process.

3. *Objectivity* = **Integrity, Accountability, and Independence:** With commitment to integrity and accountability, internal auditing provides value to governing bodies and senior management as an objective source of independent advice.[2]

Articulating Internal Audit's Value

Internal auditors often don't have a clear sense of how to articulate the value of their services. You may think internal audit's value is obvious, but sometimes stakeholders need help connecting the dots so they can see how our work relates to the value it generates. Since moving from the government to the corporate sector, I have been privileged to work with some outstanding internal audit departments whose CAEs clearly understood how to demonstrate value. But others still have difficulty articulating internal audit's value to their stakeholders.

I worked a few years ago with an internal audit department in the energy sector that produced an annual report on the department's accomplishments. The report not only summarized the unit's annual assessment of the company's risks, it included the results of key audits and highlighted some of the more proactive assistance that it had given management and the board of directors, such as helping managers with their own self-assessments and risk assessments. The report noted some of the risks that had been exposed during the past year because of its activities and reiterated the savings realized by implementing its more significant audit recommendations. It also looked ahead, outlining key risks facing the industry and the company going forward. In addition, the entire package was visually compelling and impeccably produced.

Such a document by itself doesn't demonstrate internal audit's value to an organization. But it does help certain stakeholders to see clearly the important role internal audit plays in ensuring the effectiveness of an organization's risk management and internal controls.

Delivering Value to Our Stakeholders

The value proposition is critical to understanding the core of what our stakeholders today expect from internal audit. But the value proposition alone cannot ensure that we deliver the services that best fulfill our stakeholders' needs and expectations.

Sometimes stakeholders are looking for assurance, sometimes they are looking for insight, and sometimes they are looking for an assessment. The stakeholders will ultimately define the value of their internal auditors based on how well the auditors fulfill their specific expectations. Every internal audit operation today must develop a strategy for delivering on those specific expectations. Unless internal audit can do this, it faces the risk of an emerging gap where stakeholder expectations of value are concerned.

"Can the profession seize its rightful role in risk management, governance, and compliance?" asks Rick Telberg, editor-at-large for the American Institute of Certified Public Accountants (AICPA). "Maybe, but it'll take vision and guts. Do you have what it takes in the post-meltdown world of the new normal?"[3]

In an online editorial about governance, risk, and compliance, Telberg cites responses to this question from others in the profession, including this:

Researchers at PwC report that internal auditors are being challenged "to remain relevant and meet stakeholder demands" in ways like never before.[4]

Brian Brown, PwC principal and Internal Audit Advisory Services leader, says, "What's required today is a whole new, and somewhat unnerving, concept of the internal auditor....More than simply checking accounts, internal auditors need to adopt a new way of thinking about their job that goes beyond audit as we've known it and embraces the fast-developing body of knowledge in governance, risk, and compliance." Or else, Brown says, "they run the risk of becoming marginalized and obsolete as new risk-management professionals take over.[5]

Internal auditors have been told in the past that they need to develop "soft" skills, create a "client-service culture," "leverage technology," and "promote improvement and innovation." That all may still be true, but more is needed. PwC researchers note that today's internal auditors talk more about identifying "critical risks," "aligning internal audit's value position with its stakeholder's expectations," and "matching the staffing model with that value proposition."[6]

A recent IIA Global Internal Audit survey revealed the five roles that internal auditors expect to see grow the most going forward.[7]

Internal Audit Role	Respondents Expecting Increase
Operational auditing	47%
Regulatory compliance	50%
Governance	65%
Risk management	80%
Review of financial processes	41%

With risk management, governance, and regulatory compliance atop the growth list, today's CAEs need to sit down with their internal audit staff and develop a comprehensive strategic plan that takes these areas into account.

I did something very much like this when I was hired as inspector general of TVA in 2000. I spent a couple of days when I first started to work with my senior staff to develop a very forward-looking view of the organization.

LIFE LESSON #14

It is the CAE's responsibility to develop with his or her team a comprehensive strategic plan for providing real value to internal audit's stakeholders and meeting their expectations.

The Internal Audit Strategy

The IIA's Practice Guide, Developing the Internal Audit Strategic Plan, is an excellent resource for an internal audit team creating a strategic plan for meeting its stakeholders' expectations. This section highlights some of the information from that practice guide and provides important information for development of your plan.[8]

This strategy is fundamental to internal audit remaining relevant within its organization; with it, internal auditors can adapt to stakeholders' changing expectations and realign themselves with the organization's changing objectives.

A systematic and structured process, similar to the one I used at TVA, should be used to develop the internal audit strategic plan. The following steps are offered for consideration in the practice guide:

1. Understand the organization's objectives, as well as those of the industry in which it resides.

2. Identify all of your stakeholders.

3. Learn all you can about your stakeholders' expectations, particularly those of your primary stakeholders.

4. Perform a strengths, weaknesses, opportunities, and threats (SWOT) analysis for internal auditing.

5. Update the internal audit department's vision and mission.

6. Define the critical success factors for internal audit to achieve its vision.

7. Identify the key initiatives needed to bridge the gaps that exist between where internal audit is versus where it should be.

It is important that CAEs vet their strategic plans with key stakeholders and obtain endorsement from the organization's board (or its audit committee); this is part of the CAE's obligation to report periodically to senior management and the board on internal audit's purpose, authority, responsibility, and performance (Standard 2060: Reporting to Senior Management and the Board).

Once a strategic plan for meeting stakeholders' expectations exists, it must be reviewed periodically. Factors influencing the frequency of these reviews include:

- Change in the organization's strategy.

- The organization's rate of growth and degree of maturity.

- The degree to which the organization and its senior management rely on internal audit for independent assessment of, or help managing, organizational risks.

- Significant change in internal audit resources.

- Significant change in relevant laws or significant change to organizational policies and procedures.

- The degree of change in the organization's control environment.

- Key changes in an organization's leadership team or the composition of its board of directors.

- Evaluations of how internal audit has qualitatively or quantitatively delivered on its strategic plan.

- Results of other internal/external assessments of internal audit.

While there is no way to mitigate all risk, an internal audit team can proactively manage its risks with a strategic plan. Each time I have assumed the role of CAE somewhere, I have taken my internal audit or inspector general team through a strategic planning initiative.

Strategic Planning and Value

I have emphasized strategic planning in this chapter because it is an excellent way for internal audit to identify, produce, and assess the value it should be delivering to its stakeholders. As noted earlier, however, stakeholder expectations continuously shift and so must our search for the appropriate value proposition for internal audit.

Leaders of the high-performing internal audit teams that I've become familiar with during my career were not content to merely meet stakeholder expectations as they delivered value, they were always looking for ways to exceed them. Identifying and monitoring stakeholders' needs, however, also requires the ability to develop and sustain strong relationships, a subject we will explore next.

CHAPTER 5

Relationship Acumen Is Essential to Success

Whatever success I might have enjoyed as a CAE, I might have missed out entirely on the opportunity to become one if not for my ability to cultivate and sustain relationships.

When Bernie Shell decided to retire as Chief of Internal Review for the U.S. Army Forces Command in 1988, I was astounded to learn that FORSCOM's controller had recommended me to the chief of staff as a candidate to replace Bernie. At first glance, I was an improbable choice. Although I had worked twice for Bernie in Internal Review, I had also left twice to pursue opportunities elsewhere. Now I was a senior cost analyst in another part of the command with little day-to-day interaction with the controller, who was a brigadier general.

But I also was president of the local chapter of the American Society of Military Comptrollers (ASMC), and in that capacity I had established a relationship with FORSCOM's controller and other senior FORSCOM officials. The controller had been able to observe the relationships I had developed with others throughout that organization and had apparently concluded it was a much-needed skill that I could bring to FORSCOM Internal Review.

My FORSCOM experience would repeat itself twelve years later at the U.S. Postal Service. As the USPS deputy inspector general, I had supported the IG in building and sustaining a relationship with the USPS audit committee. Following a routine committee meeting in early 2000, the audit chairman pulled me aside and asked if I would be interested in taking over as interim IG of TVA in his home state of Tennessee. TVA needed an inspector general who could forge a solid working relationship with the federal authority's board and senior management; it was in the midst of a very public feud at the time, with the board chairman having improperly accused the IG of ethical misconduct. When I acknowledged interest in the job, the USPS audit committee chairman told TVA's board members that I would be a strong choice. The rest, as they say, is history.

I share these stories not to toot my own horn but to illustrate how vital the building and maintaining of relationships can be in leading a successful internal audit operation and advancing one's career.

Internal auditors must juggle a variety of often-conflicting relationships with various stakeholders as they work to meet their responsibilities to the organizations they serve. Typically, the internal audit function is accountable to the organization's audit committee and one of its senior executives—often the CEO. But to fulfill all of the responsibilities outlined in their charters, internal auditors must also develop and maintain strong, constructive relationships with other managers and business-unit personnel within the organization and must collaborate with external auditors, compliance experts, and others. All of these stakeholder relationships require a conscious, ongoing effort to ensure the organization's risks are being appropriately identified and evaluated.[1]

You can't start too early in your career learning how to build and sustain positive, fruitful relationships with your peers and stakeholders. If you truly expect to contribute meaningfully to an organization, you have to cultivate relationships based on genuineness of character so others are confident that you are truly trying to help them—not just yourself.

The Relationship Advantage

As CAEs find themselves in an ever more visible, pressure-packed role, many have come to realize that business and financial acumen are not enough. Relationship acumen is now also essential to success.

Given many internal auditors' background in accounting, the profession isn't exactly known for its interpersonal savvy. As corporations increasingly view the CAE role as critical, some are looking beyond the walls of internal audit when filling the job, often making it a short-term, rotational post for executive development. These non-traditional CAEs, armed with broader organizational experience, often exhibit impressive relationship-building skills to complement their deep knowledge of the business.

CAEs certainly need strong relationship skills. As previously noted, most have dual reporting structures—to the CEO, CFO, or another C-level officer (administratively) and to the audit committee (functionally)—and so they must craft effective relationships with both. That can mean navigating complex and competing agendas for key stakeholders as well as the needs of external auditors, regulators, and others. If management wants its CAE to serve as a business partner or consultant—which is increasingly the case—but the board is looking for an adviser and source of assurance on the overall effectiveness of risk management and internal controls, then the CAE must somehow fulfill these seemingly conflicting roles while maintaining strong working relationships with all concerned.

Successful CAEs acknowledge that these competing expectations can be uncomfortable and stress-inducing. On one hand, the CAE must be a keen observer and assessor of organizational risks, which requires the kind of access that comes only from a close working relationship with management. On the other, this same CAE must remain objective and guard the organizational independence of the internal audit function—a task that inevitably results in occasional unflattering, if not damaging, reports about the performance of business units under the direction of senior executives. Such conflicts can easily erode relationships. Nearly everyone associated with internal audit knows of a highly respected CAE whose career was upended by conflicts with senior members of corporate management.

During my journey on the audit trail, I have made relationship building a priority in every position I held, whether the relationships were with members of the organization's audit committee, its top executives, or other staff, including those in internal audit. I have seen both the rewards of positive relationships and the severe consequences of poor or toxic relationships.

No matter how strong your relationship acumen (or how strong you think it is), you are likely to encounter situations that require you to step back and reexamine your approach. In 1998, I joined the U.S. Postal Service as deputy assistant inspector general for audit. After 10 years as a CAE, I suddenly found myself as a mid-level manager in a much bigger pond. In early meetings with staff members, I was unconsciously providing one-on-one coaching and direction, using the same tone and approach that I had employed in my prior role as a CAE in the military. Word quickly got back to the IG, who was determined to cultivate a team-based culture in the USPS void of individual egos. She quickly signaled her concern about the feedback she was getting.

The next few months were a challenge for me, as I sought to fit into this new and very different culture. I even considered going back to the Pentagon, where I had built and sustained relationships for years. But a light came on eventually; I realized that I could not begin adding real value to the Postal Service or the inspector general's office if I did not adapt my relationship-building skills to my new environment.

I started by leveraging the USPS team report-editing process (more on this later) to get to know and better understand the staff, managers, and peer executives in this non-military culture. As a result, I succeeded in winning the respect and trust of many of those who had been skeptical when I first arrived. And as I succeeded in building stronger relationships within the organization, the IG took note. She became much more supportive and began to make use of my knowledge, skills, and abilities on an ongoing basis. Within a year, she had promoted me to the assistant IG for audit, and within two years, I was the organization's deputy inspector general. Although I didn't see it at the time, my initial struggles were the result of my taking relationship acumen for granted. No matter how strong you think your relationship skills are, you must be prepared to learn new ones.

LIFE LESSON #15

Relationship skills that work in one organization may not work in another.

The Relationship Triangle

Deloitte uses a triangle to describe the relationship between internal audit, executive management, and an organization's audit committee. In a report titled *The Broken Triangle*, it noted, "The disconnect between internal audit, executive management, and the audit committee is nothing new. The broken triangle has existed for decades at many organizations, with varying degrees of severity."

Dysfunction deemed tolerable in the 1980s, 1990s, and 2000s is unacceptable today. The stakes—both personal and corporate—have ratcheted upward to new levels. Regulators, analysts, stakeholders, and even litigators all have a keen interest in how well this corporate trio, so essential to good governance and effective risk management, works together to protect and propel their organization.

What are the symptoms of a broken triangle? The Deloitte report includes:

- Financial restatements

- Material weaknesses

- Regulatory noncompliance

- Contentious or ineffectual board meetings

- Voluntary and involuntary turnover

- Missed earnings

- Excessive litigation

- Failed partnerships and alliances

- Unmitigated risk

Deloitte maintains that the first move to mend the triangle should be taken by the CAE, which may require adopting a more assertive role than in the past. The CAE should ensure that management and the audit committee have a clear view of internal audit's activities and are full partners in development of the unit's objectives, audit plan, and related activities.

The Deloitte report also offers 11 practical steps for restoring harmony to your triangle:

1. Communicate: Be open about the relationships between internal audit, the audit committee, and executive management.

2. Check your reporting lines: Determine whether your current reporting structure for the CAE is optimal.

3. Rebrand: Consider renaming your internal audit group as "audit services" or another, more descriptive and appropriate name.

4. Align expectations: Ensure that internal audit's audit plan and areas of strategic focus are understood and agreed upon by all parties.

5. Manage expectations: There's no such thing as perfect assurance.

6. Embrace risk: Expand your attention to risks that can impede your growth and profitability objectives.

7. Define internal audit's identity: Cop, detective, or counsel?

8. Expand your audit scope: Address emerging issues and trends.

9. Take control of your budget: Can you do more with less?

10. Adopt a workable model: Determine what fits best for your organization: In-house? Co-source? Outsource?

11. Make the CAE an officer: Bestow a title that helps garner the respect accorded to those in leadership positions.[2]

All internal auditors should strive to build strong relationships with the people they audit. It takes time, but our ability to have candid discussions with managers on difficult subjects can make all the difference if a manager is faced with the choice of sharing important information with us—or covering up the problem until the internal auditor leaves town. While there certainly are exceptions—fraud examinations and other specialized engagements, for instance—your audit results will almost always benefit from you having already established candid, effective working relationships with the individuals you are auditing.

Attributes That Add Up for CAEs

In 2011, I co-authored a report, *The Relationship Advantage: Maximizing Chief Audit Executive Success*, with Charles Eldridge, Paula Park, and Ellen Williams, senior executives in the research arm of the global talent management firm Korn/Ferry International. We spoke to more than a dozen executives from the field as well as some audit committee chairs. It goes without saying that strong technical audit skills and business acumen remain essential skills for today's

CAEs. But the attributes and skills that collectively we termed *relationship acumen* benefit CAEs in specific ways:

1. *Positive intent:* A fair, independent, and objective approach to the job that projects the CAE has everyone's best interest at heart. Makes clear that he or she isn't set on being right, but is set on finding the right answer.

2. *Diplomacy:* Direct, forthright communication (including listening) skills, political astuteness, and sensitivity to the organization's culture and how things get done. CAEs need to be intuitive about people and have the ability to read an audience. The best can be skillfully contrarian without being confrontational.

3. *Prescience:* Spotting the risks ahead requires curiosity, an ability to see matters with fresh eyes, and a willingness to question assumptions. Top CAEs can "see around corners"—that is, they anticipate needs before they are felt by others, and identify issues before they arise.

4. *Trustworthiness:* A CAE must always walk the talk, keep confidences, operate with integrity, and be mindful of maintaining credibility with those he or she advises. While consistency and predictability may sound boring, they're desirable qualities in this job.

5. *Leadership:* A CAE must set the tone for the entire internal audit staff, to be sure. But he or she must also be able to steer others toward consensus, manage conflict, and gain alignment on issues.

6. *Empathy:* CAEs must be able to understand and focus on each stakeholder's point of view, and be sensitive to those needs and feelings. He or she must listen. A

genuine caring about others amplifies all the other qualities on this list.[3]

Applying Relationship Acumen

Our professional standards require that we be objective, but that doesn't mean we can't be human. Other people already have a tendency to see internal auditors as cold and impersonal. I say it is incumbent upon us to change this stereotype by:

1. Acknowledging that it exists, and

2. Actively working to change it by honing our people skills.

The importance of placing our humanity ahead of our credentials when building professional relationships was best demonstrated for me during my first encounter with Gen. Colin Powell in the late 1980s, just prior to his appointment as chairman of the Joint Chiefs of Staff.

As FORSCOM Chief of Internal Review in Atlanta, I always briefed the commanding generals when they came on board. When one of these four-star generals—the highest ranking officers in the U.S. military—assumed command of FORSCOM, his staff would place me on his calendar, and on the appointed day, at the appointed hour, I would report to the general's office and brief him on the command's internal review program and the operations of its internal review office.

But when Gen. Powell, who needed to oversee a joint command like FORSCOM before he could serve as chairman of the Joint Chiefs of Staff, arrived at headquarters in 1989, they did not schedule me for a meeting in his office. "He will come to you," they said. The day of my briefing, the general came all the way over to meet with me in the dinghy, the fifty-year-old wooden structure that held our offices. It was one of many relationship-building lessons I learned from Gen. Powell.

The four-star general sat at my desk while I briefed him on what Internal Review did for FORSCOM. Later during that briefing or a subsequent one (I'm not sure which), I brought up the reductions in staff that were occurring throughout the command. The Cold War was ending, military spending was being reined in, and Army commanders were cutting budgets, including Internal Review's. At FORSCOM, the cuts were beginning to hurt Internal Review's ability to carry out its mission.

Gen. Powell looked at me and said, "All right, Dick." (He was one of the only people to ever call me Dick.) "What do we need to be concerned about?" he continued. "Tell me what I really need to be concerned about in this situation."

The general was giving me permission to level with him, to explain what kind of real risks the budget cuts might pose to his command.

LIFE LESSON #16

You will build better business relationships if you deemphasize the trappings of office and downplay rank when discussing issues of mutual concern with others.

Despite the stereotypes, internal auditors—*and the people we audit*—are first and foremost a part of humanity. It's just that, as we strive for objectivity in our work, we may sometimes accidentally flip off our *personality switches* to our detriment. It is possible to be collegial and objective at the same time—to "trust but verify," as the old expression goes.

It may help if we remember that our audit clients face exactly the same issues and challenges in their work as we do with ours. They are under the same pressures and constraints. The only difference is that, in this instance, we are not the ones being audited.

What I'm really talking about here is empathy. Submitting to an audit is an exercise in vulnerability. A little human understanding can go a long way toward changing the way people view the process and the auditors responsible for it. Remember, the goal is to improve the organization, and that's usually easier to do when everyone works together.

ESTABLISHING RAPPORT WITH YOUR SKEPTICAL CLIENTS

I have engaged more than a few skeptical or adversarial internal audit clients in my time, and so I developed five simple strategies for disarming them or winning them over:

1. *Under-promise and over-deliver.* Good relationships grow when people keep their promises to each other, and we can avoid adding to the rolls of disappointed audit clients by not promising results we're not sure we can deliver. If you're not sure when the audit report will be approved, for example, don't promise a report "next month." If you're not sure how long the audit will continue, say so. If you promise to limit your team's on-site presence to a specific time frame, make every effort to keep that promise. Of course, if your team discovers significant problems or potential fraud, all bets are off.

2. *Practice the fine art of appreciation.* Thanking clients for their time at the beginning and end of an audit is obligatory—but if you are not showing appreciation for your clients throughout the process, you are missing opportunities to turn adversaries into supporters. It's particularly important to show your appreciation when you are not in agreement. If a client questions your findings or criticizes your audit, for example, start by saying, "Thank you so much for sharing your perspectives. How would you recommend we word that instead?"

3. *Don't dwell on the past.* Clients can't undo the past, so it helps to keep conversations forward-looking. How? Limit the use of phrases like "should have" and "failed" in your client meetings and audit reports. Instead, use phrases like "from now on" or "in the future." By doing so, you are repositioning internal audits, often perceived as "fault finders" focused on past mistakes, as forward-looking reports focused on future improvements.

4. *Lend an ear.* We all know that listening is an important component of communication, but auditors too often forget that just because you now understand your client's point of view doesn't mean the client is finished talking about it. Internal audits often dredge up troublesome issues, and when clients push back, it's often because they don't think you have heard them out or truly understand their position.

5. *Try to conclude with consensus.* The best way to transform a skeptical client is to consistently strive for consensus. A few simple words such as, "Let's see if we can't find some common ground!" can diffuse a confrontational discussion and demonstrate your collaborative attitude. If, after extensive discussion, your client still vehemently disagrees with your conclusions, you should probably offer to reevaluate your conclusions to allow for a "cooling-off period." Ultimately, the two sides may agree to disagree, but clients almost always appreciate an effort to reach consensus on an audit's results.

LIFE LESSON #17

We don't always agree with those we are auditing, but we should always demonstrate through our words and actions that they have been heard and their words considered.

Client relationships, though often based on trust built over a period of time, are still very delicate. Skeptical clients often had a bad experience with internal auditors in a past life. Unfortunately, the best we can do in such cases is work tirelessly to erase the memories of those bad encounters and replace them with a new relationship built on trust.

Forging a Bond with the Audit Committee Chair

Many CAEs will tell you that their regularly scheduled annual, quarterly, or monthly meetings with the chair of their board's audit committee are simply a starting point for their relationship with that key stakeholder. CAEs and chairs who establish stronger bonds tend to reap the benefits of their relationship.

Our professional standards require the CAE to communicate and interact directly with the board.[4] The CAE's regular attendance at board meetings that relate to audit activities facilitates an ongoing exchange of information that enables the CAE to be apprised of strategic and operational developments and, in turn, apprise board members of business risks and control issues at an early stage.

But forging bonds with the chair of the audit committee should extend beyond interactions at formal meetings. Between those meetings, the CAE should remain in close, transparent, and informal communication with audit committee members—particularly the committee's chair—so that any questions or issues that arise can be addressed in timely fashion.

In my experience leading external quality assessments over the years, CAEs of high-performing internal audit departments often have a strong relationship with their audit committee chairs. These relationships often extend beyond the formal audit committee meetings. These CAEs frequently reach out between meetings to touch base on the department's performance or the risks its staff is addressing. Strong CEOs and CFOs are typically comfortable with this type of interaction, because they understand that internal audit has responsibilities that extend beyond reporting directly to them.

Audit committees can be very dynamic in terms of membership turnover. The same can be true of the chair's role. CAEs must continuously cultivate new relationships as committee members or chairs come and go. That means adapting to new styles and expectations on a continuous basis. My advice to CAEs preparing for the arrival of a new audit committee member or chair: do your homework. Make sure you research a new member's background and experience; it will help you better anticipate their frame of reference. If the incoming member serves on audit committees of other companies, reach out to the CAEs in those companies for insights and perspectives on the new member. I frequently see CAEs from two or more companies develop strong relationships with each other because they share a common audit committee member or chair.

Relationships with Management

Internal auditors walk a fine line. We are responsible for performing our mission and for maintaining both our personal objectivity and the internal audit unit's independence while simultaneously maintaining good working relationships with management. Key to managing these relationships are communicating effectively, employing participative auditing techniques, and resolving conflicts constructively.

Internal auditors are encouraged to be problem-solving partners of business unit managers to help them improve their operations; however, they also have a responsibility to remain alert for management inefficiency, ineptitude, or even fraud. They are urged to work together in participative teamwork with business unit managers, but they are often required to report deficiencies to those managers' superiors.[5]

During my career as a CAE, I found that being fair, candid, and consistent was the best recipe for maintaining effective relationships with management. They may be frustrated or disappointed the first time you issue a report critical of their operations, but if your reports are balanced and consistent over time, strong executives will learn to respect the role you must play within the organization.

Developing Your Own Relationship Acumen

The abilities that got you the CAE job—observing, absorbing, probing, listening—should also be applied to your own development.

Behavioral scientists have made strides in the past decade decoding the personal attributes that lead to strong professional relationships. Daniel Coleman's seminal work, *Emotional Intelligence*, brought these types of "EQ" skills into stark relief alongside the more "technical" skills prized within many corporate functions.[6] Korn/Ferry has a development plan for ensuring an individual's next-level readiness that it calls the "70-20-10" rule. "The formula for developing successful executives is quite clear: 70 percent of development comes from experience, 20 percent from feedback and people, and 10 percent from courses or training events."[7]

Following almost ten years as an internal auditor, I ventured away from the profession in 1984 and accepted a post as an operations research analyst. Because of the educational qualifications generally required in operations research, I found myself suddenly surrounded by professionals with degrees in mathematics who possessed skill sets completely different from mine. To say I was intimidated was an understatement. For the next three years, I would find myself constantly challenged to measure up to their extraordinary background and training.

To ensure my success in this new role, I scheduled myself for extensive professional and academic training. I suspect that I overcompensated out of a fear of failure. In the end, I was promoted within the field and ended up leading several important projects.

Some years earlier, in 1978, I had finished my MBA and wanted to do something with my graduate degree, so I looked into teaching accounting. In the spring of 1980, I began to teach accounting and economics courses at Clayton Community College just outside of Atlanta. When I walked into class my first night, I was mortified; I had never done anything like this before, and as I stood at the front of the class with my class notes, I was gripping the podium very tightly. A lot of Vietnam War veterans were still seeking educations, and I was by far the youngest person in the room. It was all just a little bit intimidating for a twenty-five-year-old. But I quickly learned to build relationships with my students by being myself and getting to know them as people. I quickly discovered how much I loved it. I taught for eight years, and those classroom experiences made me much more comfortable when getting to know new people or speaking in front of large groups. I've had a passion for training and education ever since.

LIFE LESSON #18

*Whether building relationships or taking on a role for which I have little experience, I discovered throughout my career that the absolutely greatest motivator for me to strive for success is **fear of failure**. I always thrive and do the best if I maintain a healthy fear of failure.*

Long-Term Care

Successful CAEs understand that, even in the best of circumstances, the process of building and sustaining relationships is a never-ending task. Senior executives come and go or change hats, and the audit committee roster changes. The CAE must reach out early and often when personnel change. Tending to long-standing relationships is also imperative. Picking up the phone or extending a lunch invitation to talk through a touchy issue pays enormous dividends to the CAE and the entire internal audit staff.

Building trust and understanding in others requires an investment of the CAE's time and energy, in part because the needs and expectations of key stakeholders are constantly evolving. Successful CAEs recognize the signs of change and recalibrate.

Establishing and maintaining important allegiances changes the entire CAE experience. Having the audit chair as an ally gains the CAE credibility with the whole committee and inspires respect from management.

In the long run, success depends on a balanced mix of relationship acumen and the ability to identify risks—and then using the results as a basis for audit planning and internal audit value creation.

CHAPTER 6

When in Doubt, Follow the Risk

Early in my career, the word *risk* rarely came up during my internal audit activities. In deciding what to do, we typically developed an "audit universe," consisting of all of the operating units, business entities, organizational processes, and controls that were our responsibility, then we used that universe as our "audit register" to ensure that each area was assessed on a predetermined schedule. For example, the Army's officers' clubs had to be audited every three years by regulation, whether they needed it or not. By the time I became a chief audit executive (CAE) in the late 1980s, those cyclical requirements were largely gone, though they were still very much a force of habit.

By the late 1990s, however, internal auditors had begun to focus on risk as an important determining factor when developing their audit plans and allocating resources. We began experimenting with risk assessments as part of the audit-planning process when I was the assistant inspector general for audit at the Postal Service. I still recall the IG and I informally chronicling our view of the USPS' risks on the back of a napkin en route to an international postal conference in China in 1999. Preparing risk assessments and using the results to develop a comprehensive audit plan was still generally viewed as a leading practice at the time, so we were proud of our preliminary efforts.

By the time I moved to the Tennessee Valley Authority (TVA) as inspector general in the summer of 2000, the Postal Service Office of Inspector General (OIG) had completed its second risk assessment, and I thought of myself as a fast-developing expert on risk-based audit planning. So when I showed up at TVA headquarters in Knoxville, Tennessee, I was confident I already knew the key risks facing the giant power authority—and was certain the first audit plan under my direction would focus extensively on the risks posed by TVA's nuclear power plants.

So imagine my surprise when, after several days of meetings with my audit team, the risk assessment identified the authority's contracting processes for acquiring coal as the biggest risk. Buying coal riskier than operating nuclear power plants? What I hadn't realized was that TVA's OIG staff had been using risk-based planning for its audits prior to my arrival—and had a much better understanding of TVA's risks than I did.

I began to appreciate that risk has at least two dimensions—likelihood and impact. While even a single accident at a nuclear power plant could be catastrophic in terms of its effect on the organization, the environment, and the surrounding community, the likelihood of such an accident was relatively remote given the oversight track record of the U.S. Nuclear Regulatory Commission and other regulatory bodies, coupled with the extraordinary safety, security, and operating controls that were in place.

Meanwhile, TVA spent billions of dollars annually buying coal, the fuel responsible for generating most of the electrical power used by its customers. Not only did wasteful, ineffective, or even fraudulent coal-acquisition practices have the potential to cost TVA and its ratepayers lots of money—but the likelihood of those things occurring in the coal-contracting processes was high as well.

So high impact combined with high likelihood trumped high impact with low likelihood. I also learned that this risk-based approach can add real value to an organization. During my tenure at TVA, we identified more deficiencies, cost recoveries, and cost savings from our coal-contract audits and investigations than from all of the other audits in my entire career—combined!

The Fundamentals of Risk

In 2002, The IIA adopted its first standards mandating that risk assessments serve as the basis for audit planning. While serving as vice president of The IIA's Learning Center in 2003, I delivered a two-day lecture in China on risk assessment in audit planning. During my years at PricewaterhouseCoopers (PwC), I worked with the internal audit units of several Fortune 500 companies to enhance their risk assessment and audit planning processes. Regardless of the approach, there was one overarching principle taking hold in the profession: make sure internal auditing follows the risks.

While risk and risk management are relatively new to internal auditing, they are not new to the world of commerce. In his book, *Against the Gods: The Remarkable Story of Risk*, Peter L. Bernstein writes that systematically understanding the risk factors affecting business has been a goal for millennia. Among his examples:

- Advancement of the theory of probability, in use since the mid-seventeenth century to explain outcomes in games of chance

- Risk transfer and distribution practices that Chinese and Babylonian traders used as early as the third and second centuries BC.

- Historical records of financial loans in Babylon dating back to the eighteenth century BC.[1]

Business risk is defined multiple ways in the twenty-first century. The Committee of Sponsoring Organizations of the Treadway Commission (COSO), for example, defines risk as: "...the possibility that an event will occur and adversely affect the achievement of an objective."[2] Other definitions take a more holistic view of risk and recognize that there can be a positive dimension as well. Still, it is safe to say that most internal auditors today focus on the potential bad consequences when assessing risk.

The Importance of Risk Assessment

Just a few years ago, annual risk assessments were considered a leading practice but were not required under The IIA's International Professional Practices Framework (IPPF). Today, documented risk assessments are mandated at least once a year.

In working with different internal audit departments over the years, I have observed that, even if internal auditors vary their approach, certain features are common to the development of their risk-based plans. These include:

- The establishment and maintenance of a risk register or inventory for the organization, linked to key business objectives

- The assignment of an inherent rating for risks in the inventory

- A process for scoring or rating risks on an annual basis

- A process for gathering and analyzing data, management perspectives, and other evidence on the current level of risk for each element in the inventory

- A scoring or rating methodology that is assigned based on the data, perspective, and evidence gathered

- A ranking or prioritization of risks based on the scoring methodology

- A determination of the most highly rated risks to be included in the proposed internal audit plan

- A review of the proposed annual internal audit plan with key management officials

- Submission of the proposed annual internal audit plan to the audit committee for approval

Over the years, I have seen elaborate, time-consuming methodologies, including formulas used to score individual risks. Sometimes these formulas seemed better suited for a rocket launch than calculating a single risk in an audit plan. As I often coach internal auditors, simplified formulas can be just as effective as complicated ones. After all, risk assessment is as much art as science; no matter how complex the process, professional judgment will invariably be a factor.

THE VALUE OF RISK ASSESSMENT TO STAKEHOLDERS

While the primary purpose of most internal audit departments' risk assessment process is to generate a basis for the annual audit plan, its value to internal audit's stakeholders cannot be overstated. In the early years of risk-based planning by internal audit, managements tended to find the assessment process and outcome useful, but audit committees typically received little exposure to it. However, in recent years, audit committees have taken more direct oversight of internal audit in many organizations. Before approving internal audit's annual plan, audit committee members naturally want to know the basis for prioritization of key internal audits for the year ahead. The more they see, the more they often want to be involved. Today, many internal audit departments will include interviews with audit committee members as an integral part of the risk assessment process.

Internal auditors spend a great deal of time and resources to undertake an annual risk assessment. For large internal audit departments of sizable organizations, the effort can represent hundreds of staff hours. Often, the risk assessment itself is then filed away as an evidence of the planning process for possible review during a subsequent external quality assessment of the department. However, I believe internal auditors miss a significant opportunity to deliver value by not sharing the risk assessment with management. In fact, I have received favorable response from management and audit committee members by packaging the risk assessment results as an engagement deliverable—similar to an internal audit report. When internal audit is seen as the enterprise expert in risk management, its annual risk assessment can serve as an important reference document for the entire organization.

Internal audit pioneered enterprise risk assessments at many companies. As managements and boards placed greater importance on enterprise risk management (ERM) during the past decade, many turned to internal audit to leverage its expertise. In some companies, internal audit departments were asked to champion or implement ERM, and the CAE was asked to wear a second hat—that of chief risk officer (CRO). While such moves reflect stakeholders' growing confidence in internal audit, the long-term consequences of internal audit retaining responsibility for ERM are not without risk, because its ability to serve as an objective source of assurance on the effectiveness of risk management for the organization could be compromised. After all, internal auditors should never audit their own work.

Where Is the Risk Taking Us?

The IIA's Audit Executive Center conducted an annual survey in recent years to assess key trends in the profession. Since 2012, the survey has also sought to document which categories of risk internal audit spends most of its risk-coverage resources. An average of the recent surveys' results provides interesting insights as to which risks are getting the most attention—and which are getting the least.[3]

The average results of recent surveys reflect several recent and important trends. First, the results reveal that internal audit is looking at a broad portfolio of risks—one that arguably contains many of the risks that organizations face today. Of course, that should not be surprising given the risk-based approach that most internal audit functions pursue in developing their annual audit plans.

Risk Category	Average time spent per risk category
Operational	26%
Compliance and regulatory	15%
Financial (general)	14%
Sarbanes-Oxley	12%
Information technology	11%
Strategic and business	5%
Risk management assurance	6%
Fraud	4%
Other	8%

The survey results also help dispel the myth that internal audit is primarily concerned with financial risks: only 26 percent of internal audit's risk-coverage resources are dedicated to financial risks (the "Financial General" and "Sarbanes-Oxley" categories combined). And the results reflect that when combined, more than 50 percent of internal audit's risk-related resources were dedicated to operational, compliance and regulatory, and information technology risks.

Meanwhile, only about 5 percent of internal audit's resources are dedicated to strategic business risks. While that percentage may be higher than it would have been a decade ago, it still falls short of what it should be, given two important considerations. First, The IIA Audit Executive Center's 2014 survey[4] indicated that was the risk category to which both management and audit committees were paying the most attention. The disparity between stakeholders' interest in strategic business risks and the amount of attention they were getting from internal audit could portend trouble for the profession in the form of an emerging expectations gap.

Internal audit's limited coverage of strategic business risks also contrasts with the *real risk to shareholder value* posed by that category, according to a noted PwC report. In discussing the composite results of previous studies, PwC reported that "[n]early 60% of the time, a strategic or business factor was behind rapid losses in shareholder value. The causes can vary widely, from a major product or service introduction by a competitor to the impact of a new regulation."[5] Yet despite growing evidence that strategic business risks can be lethal to twenty-first century companies, internal audit departments continue to dedicate only a small fraction of their resources to such risks. In my opinion, this remains one of many opportunities for internal auditors to provide clients with even greater added value.

Assurance on the Effectiveness of Risk Management

I have been urging the internal audit profession for some time now to provide assurance on risk management's effectiveness. I consider it the most significant opportunity for our profession in a generation, yet internal auditors seem reluctant to make such assurances an integral part of their portfolios. What are we waiting for?

There is widespread agreement that failures of risk management in the late 2000s—particularly in the financial services sector—were a major contributor to the global economic crisis. Among the legacies of that crisis are the many new regulations and laws worldwide designed to pressure corporate executives into more effectively managing their companies' risks and corporate boards into more effectively exercising their oversight responsibilities. To whom should these boards turn for assurance? Surely they cannot rely strictly on management, for management cannot be fully objective about its own performance.

The IIA is convinced that assurance on risk management is a very important issue for our profession in the decade ahead. So convinced of this is The IIA that in late 2011, it launched the certification for risk management assurance (CRMA) as a way for internal auditors to demonstrate their proficiency in providing assurance of risk management's effectiveness. The response was amazing! Within the first two years of the certification's launch, more than 13,000 internal auditors worldwide added CRMA to their résumés. By the end of 2013, it was The IIA's second-most widely held certification, behind the certified internal auditor (CIA) designation.

Despite the potential value of risk management assurance to companies and other organizations, internal audit departments dedicate very few of their resources to this emerging priority.[6] So why aren't CAEs, who play a major role in setting internal audit priorities, embracing the change? I think it is a matter of not wanting to leave one's *comfort zone*. Assurance on risk management was simply not a priority for the profession in the past, and many CAEs still don't feel comfortable taking on such a role. Meanwhile, because we do not have a history of providing assurance on the *effectiveness* of risk management, boards and management are not yet clamoring for internal audit to assume this new, broader role either.

It's ironic that all of this is occurring at a time when audit executives are appealing for a "seat at the table." Such a seat, it is argued, would afford CAEs a better understanding of their organization's key strategic and business risks. Perhaps it was a bit harsh, yet when noted thought leader Norman Marks observed on Twitter that "internal auditors who don't provide assurance on risk management deserve a seat at the 'children's table,'" I couldn't help but smile. I discuss the importance of a "seat at the table" in much greater detail in chapter 16.

Internal auditors should remember that, for many internal audit functions, access to the audit committee and its chairman is still a relatively recent development. The need for assurance on financial controls' effectiveness—which was a key priority for audit committees during the past decade—opened doors for internal audit within many organizations and raised the profile of CAEs with many audit committees and management teams. But internal auditors cannot take that for granted. For if, having realigned their audit coverage, they compensate by spending less time on issues of importance to the audit committee or management, there is a risk committee members or those in the executive suites will start to think that internal audit's work is no longer relevant.

Expanding Our Risk Horizon

For generations, accountants and auditors have disparagingly been referred to as "bean counters." If we have been guilty of counting beans, it's time to demonstrate our true capabilities and the value we bring to our organizations. It's time to move beyond *bean counting* and begin to fully comprehend *how the beans are grown*, which is often where crucial risks to an organization lie.

But many new internal auditors have little or no experience with operational auditing, having spent most of their time focused on financial controls. How do they develop their business acumen generally and their understanding of the specific risks in the businesses and industries in which they operate? I suggest the following:

- *Become a "sponge" for information about the business.* Read and learn everything you can about your organization and the industry in which it operates. While a typical U.S. Securities and Exchange Commission (SEC) 10-K report for a publicly traded company can be dry reading, it is a *treasure chest* of information about your company and the strategic risks it faces.

- *Seek variety in your assignments.* While it is great to become an expert in a specific area of a business' operations, you will be even more valuable as a resource if your expertise spans multiple areas.

- *Be passionate about every assignment.* During my years in the Postal Service's OIG, I came to realize that the new auditors who truly impressed management were the ones with the enthusiasm and drive to quickly become conversant enough in business risks and controls to talk with twenty-year veterans.

- *Rotate into other areas of the business.* As much as we would like to think we can learn everything we need to know about a business while wearing our internal audit hat, there is no substitute for hands-on experience. My foray into operations research and cost analysis in the 1980s made me a much better internal auditor when I returned to the profession.

- *Seek training or other professional development to fill gaps in your knowledge.* I relayed in the last chapter how, as the newly appointed inspector general of TVA, I enrolled in a basic utilities course so I could better understand the fundamentals of generating and distributing electric power. No one ordered me to do it, but I realized I needed to know more about the business if I was to succeed as the newly appointed CAE.

- *Be patient.* Learning all you should about a business and sharpening your business acumen overall takes time.

LIFE LESSON #19

Look at all of the enterprise risks facing your organization. If you focus on just certain ones, such as financial risks, you will fall short of your potential as an internal auditor and risk placing your internal audit department and the overall organization in peril.

By the time I left the Postal Service in 2000, the OIG had more than 500 staff, and yet I still felt like we had to conserve our resources because we were trying to audit one of the largest enterprises in the world—responsible for moving 40 percent of the world's mail through 38,000 post offices employing almost a million workers combined. It was only by concentrating on the most important risks facing the Postal Service that we could do the job with the limited resources available to us. If we had taken the "old school" approach of auditing everything according to a strict rotating schedule, we would have missed many of our biggest opportunities to add value to the agency.

LIFE LESSON #20

Establish risk-based criteria for prioritizing your audit coverage. Without that, you won't know where to start.

Auditing the Circus

While internal auditors often declare they can address the full portfolio of an organization's risks, skeptics still abound. I have heard many executives complain that "internal auditors just don't understand the business." My sense is that some of these complaints are legitimate, while others originate with unit managers who simply don't want internal auditors poking around in their business.

Many internal auditors hired by their organizations in recent years were brought on to help with enhanced coverage of risks related to financial controls. Many of the auditors in this new generation had little knowledge of their company or its industry; they were proficient in supporting activities related to the Sarbanes-Oxley Act but had little—if any—experience in auditing operational risks. So it's understandable that internal audit's efforts to cover a broader portfolio of risks has exposed some internal auditors' limited knowledge of their particular business.

A recent IIA Audit Executive Center survey suggested some strategies for internal auditors seeking to improve their business acumen. Almost 90 percent of those responding to the survey indicated that a good way to improve a unit's collective knowledge of the business was "internal development of existing personnel," such as:

- Subscribing to industry periodicals or other literature— 75 percent
- Training focused on industry risks or issues—69 percent
- Pairing inexperienced staff with more experienced staff— 69 percent
- Sending the CAE to industry-focused CAE groups or events—55 percent
- Networking frequently and informally with other CAEs—49 percent[7]

I am confident that, as professionals, we can always close any gaps in knowledge we may have about the businesses we work for. But there will always be executives and managers who think their business units are too complex or sophisticated for mere auditors to understand. They will push back when our risk assessments indicate that their areas of responsibility warrant internal audit coverage. If the internal auditors prevail and complete the audits, then the managers will often dispute the findings on the basis that the auditors don't have the proper expertise and don't know what they're talking about.

During my career, I have debated more than a few disgruntled managers who wanted to keep my staff out of their areas on the basis of lack of expertise. With very few exceptions, I was successful in refuting their assertions. On those occasions where there was some validity to their concerns, I typically secured the necessary expertise by co-sourcing the engagement with a third party. My advice to any CAE faced with such circumstances is to stand firm. As one of my colleagues once cleverly responded to a business-unit manager who doubted internal audit's ability to assess his operations, "You don't have to be a clown to audit the circus."

Risk-based internal auditing is challenging enough when the risks remain relatively static. But if we have learned anything during the past decade, it is that risks rarely remain still. The evolving nature of risk and the challenges that poses for internal auditors is the topic of chapter 7.

CHAPTER 7

Risk: A Moving Target

When Iraqi military forces under the command of Saddam Hussein invaded neighboring Kuwait on August 2, 1990, it was one of the more geopolitically destabilizing events in decades. Little did I realize, however, how much the invasion— unfolding more than 7,000 miles from U.S. Army Forces Command, where I was FORSCOM's Chief of Internal Review— would teach me about the ever-shifting nature of risk and about stakeholder expectations.

We had compiled the 1990 internal audit plan for our giant, Atlanta-based military command during the summer of 1989; the Berlin Wall had yet to fall and the world was a relatively peaceful place. As a result, FORSCOM's internal audit priorities were much the same as they had been in previous years. I was enjoying the support of my new boss, Maj. Gen. (MG) Robert Wiegand, and I had made sure to coordinate with him to ensure that his expectations were reflected in our plan.

But in the ensuing months, MG Wiegand would depart and be replaced by MG H.G. "Pete" Taylor. This two-star general, unlike

MG Wiegand, seemed to have little interest in internal review or our annual audit plan. He made it clear to me when he arrived at FORSCOM that he thought there were too many auditors conducting too many in his command. (Considering that, during the heart of the Gulf War, our command was the subject of as many as 140 audits by *outside* audit agencies alone, I suppose I could understand his point of view.)

I was determined to prove to MG Taylor that internal review added value to his command, and it was the Gulf War that provided me with my best opportunity. Shortly after Iraq's invasion of Kuwait, the Third U.S. Army's headquarters (located alongside FORSCOM in Atlanta) was deployed to Saudi Arabia at the invitation of the Saudi government. The deployment was so swift and sudden that the soldiers had left their personal belongings behind, unattended, in their barracks at Fort McPherson. Turns out that situation was one of many organizational risks that were probably keeping MG Taylor awake at night.

When I sat down with the general for my monthly update, I asked him point blank if there was anything internal review could do to address the command's war-related issues. He thought for a moment, then asked if our auditors could review security provisions for the barracks of those soldiers sent suddenly to the Mideast, to provide him some assurance that their personal effects were adequately secured. We immediately undertook the audit, and it was a transformational event in internal review's relationship with MG Taylor. It was also a pivotal event for me, for it deepened my understanding of how rapidly new risks can evolve in an otherwise stable organization. Risks, I realized, really are a moving target.

In the years since that important lesson, I have seen businesses worldwide focus more and more on managing risks, be they internal or external, financial, operational, technological, strategic-and-business, regulatory, or related to reputation.

Deciding how much risk should be tolerated for the sake of growth, identifying which risks must be mitigated, and uncovering hidden risks with the potential to devastate an organization can be a daunting assignment. Yet the opportunities are enormous. And who within an organization has the independent and objective perspective, the skills and experience, to identify these risks and provide assurance that they are well managed? In most organizations, the answer to that question is the internal auditors.

In the months following Iraq's invasion of Kuwait, new risks seemed to emerge weekly at FORSCOM. After internal review demonstrated its agility in addressing the security of those deployed soldiers' personal effects, we took on a series of new challenges, from auditing the logistics contracts that moved thousands of soldiers halfway around the world and back, to assessing processes for activating and deploying reserve soldiers, to studying how personal mail was being delivered within the theater of operations. We eventually identified and deployed to the Middle East a team of military internal review auditors—the first U.S. soldier-auditors to serve in combat conditions since the Vietnam War. I learned that, in a highly dynamic environment, a good CAE has to continuously be on the lookout for new risks that might warrant internal audit coverage.

No Surprises

Having had opportunities to speak with the audit committee chairmen of many leading U.S. and European corporations during the past decade, I like to ask them during our conversation, "What is your foremost expectation from internal audit?" With amazing regularity, the most common response is, "No surprises."

In other words, these audit chairmen, reflecting their personal views and those of their committees, want internal auditors to identify issues *before* they become problems for the company and appear on the front page of *The Wall Street Journal.*

If you stop to think about it, you realize "no surprises" is an extraordinary expectation. It suggests internal auditors must be omniscient. Is the eradication of unwelcome surprises what audit committees really expect from our profession? I seriously doubt it. Instead, I think they are urging internal audit to anticipate risks that could present a problem down the road, rather than dwelling only on what has already gone wrong. To do that, internal auditors need to recognize that risk is a moving target—and a volatile one at that.

Which is why internal audit must take a more continuous approach to risk assessment. Audit plans and coverage should constantly evolve as new, *potential* risks surface and undergo assessment. Such an approach would add significant value for internal audit's stakeholders, particularly in the kinds of dynamic environments that accompany sudden or unexpected crises.

Methods for Continuous Risk Assessment

Conventional planning for internal auditing is not designed to identify unexpected risks. I was in the middle of just such an old-school, annual plan when Iraq invaded Kuwait in 1990. Risks suddenly reared up that virtually no one had seen coming. I had to toss my internal audit plan for the year and begin to continuously assess risks so I could identify and set our internal audit priorities.

How likely are we to avoid surprises if we follow traditional methods and routinely conduct our audits based on a plan that's six months to a year old? Not only do we need to assess risk continuously, we need to use that information to keep our audit plan up to date.

> ——————— LIFE LESSON #21 ———————
>
> *Unless we also have a robust method for continuously assessing risk, we will be caught off guard by unpleasant surprises lurking just out of sight.*

One of the most common excuses I hear from internal auditors for not designing continuous risk-assessment processes is that they are difficult and time-consuming; many departments have trouble finding time for even one enterprise-wide risk assessment each year. But several simple techniques are available to help you keep your risk assessment up to date throughout the year:

1. *Formal methods.* In its most recent Common Body of Knowledge (CBOK) Study, The IIA Research Foundation noted that "[t]he idea that an internal audit activity can update its audit plan only once a year and still remain timely, responsive, and effective needs to be challenged strongly."[1] One way to continuously monitor risk is to identify key risk indicators (KRIs) at the outset of the year and monitor them periodically or continuously throughout the year. These KRIs can be linked to the results of the annual risk assessment, or to risks that are notoriously volatile. When anomalies appear, internal audit should assess whether the organization's risks are shifting, and internal audit's coverage should adapt accordingly.

2. *Shoe-leather assessments.* Another method for keeping your risk assessment and audit plan up to date is what I like to call *risk assessment by walking around.* This method relies on developing strong working relationships with key members of senior management, so that you know about new risks as soon as they do. Risk assessment by walking around may lack the discipline and structure of more formal assessments, but it's a powerful way to keep in touch with what's happening in your organization and may reveal new risks that your formal risk indicators do not. Given the number of business units and executives in large companies, risk assessment by walking around cannot be the responsibility of the CAE alone; the entire internal audit department must be organized and deployed.

3. *Bird's-eye view.* A third approach is simply to set your antenna as high as possible to detect industry-wide changes, economic trends, and other external factors. Industry publications, seminars, and professional association meetings can be valuable sources for this type of risk assessment. This, too, must be a team effort.

So what's the best type of continuous risk-assessment program for keeping up with the speed of doing business these days? Any one of the methods just outlined is a far better option than merely establishing an audit plan once a year and then following it regardless of changing circumstances. Unfortunately, none of those methods is truly complete by itself. My advice: use a combination of methods. Formal methods are best for staying on top of previously identified risks; risk assessment by walking around helps identify new internal risks; and setting our antenna high to identify new external risks allows us to start addressing them as they emerge elsewhere in our industry or in the economy generally.

Key Action Steps for Continuously Assessing Risks

The IIA's recent CBOK Study included the need to "Conduct a More Responsive and Flexible Risk-based Audit Plan" as one of its "Imperatives for Change." The study recommended the following "Key Action Steps for CAEs:"[2]

- Assess the maturity of your risk assessment process and develop plans to extend its application across the enterprise.
- Develop processes within internal auditing to identify and report on emerging risks:
  - Make the identification of emerging issues a key performance responsibility of your direct reports.

- Coordinate with the organization's other risk and control units to share information and views on emerging issues.

- Identify and use external sources of relevant data, knowledge, and business issues to assist in the identification of external emerging issues.

■ Assess your process for making periodic updates and revisions to your annual audit plan; develop steps to enable internal auditing to move faster and make more frequent changes to the audit plan as the organization's risks change.

■ Talk to your key stakeholders (executive management and the audit committee) about the need to make more frequent updates to the audit plan; seek agreement on an appropriate balance between the need for internal auditing to "complete the annual plan" and their desire for internal auditing to make changes in response to emerging and changing risks:

- Consider implementation of a "rolling" audit plan; for example, a plan that is rolled forward to cover the next six months.

- Conduct regular, frank discussions with both senior management and the audit committee about the nature, scope, and severity of the organization's risk profile.

■ Develop or refine your audit reporting to demonstrate a more direct link between changes to the organization's risk profile and associated changes to the audit plan.

Identifying Emerging Risks

Internal auditors have become increasingly good at assessing conventional risks, but identifying and assessing emerging risks presents new challenges and requires even greater proficiency. Emerging risks, while still developing, could still pose near-term threats to an organization's business model and strategies. Because the enterprise has no track record yet in coping with these risks, they are difficult to identify and assess.

Too often, conventional risk-assessment techniques miss emerging risks completely. Even the biggest game-changing risks can be hard to spot until something bad actually occurs. Until relatively recently, for example, regulations such as the U.S. Foreign Corrupt Practices Act (FCPA) and the more recently enacted U.K. Bribery Act were largely ignored by most internal audit departments. Risks involving cloud computing were not contemplated. There was no global liquidity crisis, and relatively few city governments were in severe financial distress. Organizations that were not positioned to respond rapidly to these changing conditions often paid a high price.

Because emerging risks such as these can have devastating effects, one might think that they would receive a lot of attention and significant resources from an organization's management. But just the opposite is often the case: emerging risks are usually not yet on management's radar, and there's a tendency to avoid dealing with risks that have not yet materialized. When preoccupied with trying to solve today's problems, it is tempting to ignore risks that are still just over the horizon. As the old saying goes, "Don't worry about tomorrow, for tomorrow never comes." But tomorrow does come, and it is the ability to solve tomorrow's problems before they can occur that audit committees most value in a CAE.

LIFE LESSON #22

Internal auditors must become students of the global economic and geopolitical environment and stay informed about industry trends and the regulatory landscape if they don't want to miss emerging threats from outside the organization.

As we have seen, emerging risks can appear from any direction, from inside or outside the organization, so internal audit must have broad peripheral vision and think creatively. Simply updating last year's risk assessment won't cut it. We must truly look at the organization's goals, objectives, and operations with a fresh eye each time and constantly ask ourselves, "What could keep us from accomplishing this as intended?"

We must know what drives corporate performance and understand the factors that might hinder our organizations from executing their strategies and reaching their goals. We must develop better risk analytics, and we must evaluate how emerging risks are incorporated into strategic plans. We must be able to look at "what if" scenarios and spot potential opportunities before they have passed us by, because the only way to ensure that our audit committees are not surprised is to keep them informed of potential developments before they occur.

Competent, effective CAEs and internal audit staff may often recognize an emerging risk that has not yet been communicated to us by management. Several times during my career, I was able to find such added value and communicate it in such a way that it benefited both the organization and the relationships I had with management.

Maj. Gen. Taylor made it clear to me upon his arrival at FORSCOM in 1990 that he was no fan of auditors. Yet, once we started addressing his needs and demonstrating real value to him, he seemed to soften his views.

He didn't stay at FORSCOM for long; when he was promoted to three-star general and made one of the Army's prestigious corps commanders, a large farewell dinner was organized for him and, as a senior member of his staff, I attended. When he stood to give his farewell speech, he began going around the room directing personal comments to individuals with whom he had worked. He eventually pointed at me and said, "Chambers, you back there. I still don't like auditors, but you are welcome at my command any time." That was a capstone moment for me, and it demonstrated the value I had provided him once I recognized that risk is a moving target.

CHAPTER 8

Communication
Must Be Continuous

Throughout my career, from entry-level associate to where I sit today, effective communication has been critically important. I learned early in my tenure as a CAE that it is important to communicate not only well, but frequently, too. But in no job was this ability more important to my success than when I served as inspector general (IG) of the Tennessee Valley Authority (TVA).

TVA is a wholly owned corporation of the U.S. government. As its IG, I had some of the most important and visible stakeholders that any CAE will ever encounter. Not only did I work for TVA's Board of Directors, I also counted among my key stakeholders members of Congress and the president of the United States. Communicating with TVA's board was not a new experience for me, because I had assisted the Postal Service's inspector general in carrying out this critical responsibility as the USPS' deputy IG before moving to the power authority. But having to communicate with the likes of Congress and the White House was unchartered territory for me.

While required by law to deliver semiannual reports to all members of Congress, I knew that the lawmakers most interested in TVA were those whose constituents relied on TVA-produced electricity—a group that consisted of fourteen senators and fourteen House members.

I made a commitment early in my tenure at TVA to establish relationships with as many of these congressional stakeholders and their staffs as possible. I routinely flew from Knoxville to Washington and walked the halls of Congress to foster and sustain these important relationships. The initial rounds of visits were to introduce myself. Subsequent meetings were designed to gain a better understanding of the needs and expectations of the senators and representatives. As we delivered on the lawmakers' expectations, and the number of meetings in Washington multiplied, I began developing strong relationships with certain contacts, particularly key congressional staff members.

Just a few months after TVA's board hired me as IG, Congress added the post to the list of IGs that from then on would be appointed by the president. I expected to remain in the job until the president nominated someone for confirmation by the U.S. Senate, so I added the Office of Management and Budget (OMB), an arm of the White House, to my list of Washington stakeholders, visiting there whenever possible. In the summer of 2001, I received the long-awaited call from the White House that the president was preparing to nominate a permanent IG for TVA. While such nominees were required by law to be qualified for their appointed posts, they typically were also connected politically in some fashion. So when the caller from the Office of Presidential Personnel advised me that the president wanted to nominate me as TVA's first presidentially appointed inspector general, I was astounded. Only later did I learn that key members of Congress had weighed in with the White House to indicate their desire that I remain in the job.

Ultimately, I declined the nomination so I could retire from government and start a new career. Still, my efforts to build and sustain key relationships with members of Congress and their staffs through continuous communication had resulted, as an unintended consequence, in my becoming a nominee for appointment by the president of the United States. It's a lesson about continuous communication—learned on one of the world's biggest stages—that I have never forgotten.

Continuous communication is a struggle for many internal auditors. Many of those in the profession are introverts; communicating with other people doesn't come naturally to us. As internal audit professionals, we are often recognized for the many outstanding skills and characteristics that we bring to bear in executing our important role within businesses, government agencies, and other organizations. But our inability to communicate effectively can impede our attempts to build and maintain a rapport with stakeholders.

The IIA's 2010 Common Body of Knowledge (CBOK) survey results indicated that the core competency that stakeholders value most in an internal auditor is an ability to communicate. Nearly 86 percent of the survey's respondents rated communication skills (defined as report writing as well as oral, written, and presentation skills) as "very important."[1]

The communication starts long before an audit engagement; it begins with the relationships you cultivate with stakeholders and others within your organization (see chapter 5). When it's time to conduct the audit, you will be looking for managers and others within the company to open up to you and share details about the kinds of things that keep them awake at night, what they see as their biggest challenges, and what they want you to do to help them. If you don't have the ability to converse with these people informally and build positive relationships with them *before* you start the audit, you will find yourself at a great disadvantage during the engagement.

As a CAE, you have to make a point of having regular luncheon meetings or other social interactions with those executives. You may be uncomfortable with that—you may prefer to spend that lunch hour eating at your desk—but if you truly want to understand the vulnerabilities of your business and the risks it faces, you have to be willing to have such conversations. Effective communication is also critical to building a successful relationship with the audit committee and, ultimately, delivering value to the company.

COMMUNICATION

The internal audit professional...

1. Secures the trust of others through positive use of communication.

2. Fosters open communication.

3. Demonstrates respect for others, and customizes messages to reflect the needs of the target audience.

4. Organizes and expresses ideas clearly and with confidence in order to influence others.

5. Extracts key information from a variety of sources to support communication.

6. Selects appropriate communication forms (verbal, nonverbal, visual, written) and media (face to face, electronic, paper-based).

7. Employs the technical conventions of the language (spelling, punctuation, grammar, etc.) correctly.

8. Listens actively, asking questions as required to check one's own understanding.

9. Solicits feedback from the audience to gauge the effectiveness of the communication.

10. Anticipates reactions to communication and plans responses in advance.

11. Discusses audit findings and their impacts professionally and confidently with appropriate levels of the organization.

12. Interprets and uses body language to reinforce communication.

13. Uses graphical methods to communicate processes and other complex information.

14. Delivers information in a structured fashion to foster learning and development among members of the audience.

15. Applies appropriate communication skills in interviews.[2]

You Need Strong, Effective Communication Skills

Strong, effective communication skills—especially effective interviewing skills—are as important to your annual and internal audit engagement cycles as the planning of your engagements' tactical elements.

The ability to communicate with impact is one of ten core competencies in The IIA's Global Internal Audit Competency Framework, which defines the competencies auditors need to meet the requirements of The IIA's International Professional Practices Framework (IPPF).

The Competency Framework highlights a number of skills internal auditors must demonstrate as effective communicators. These skills are required of all internal auditors, though the need for these skills increases with your seniority on staff.

If we are going to be effective in this profession, we have to be familiar and comfortable with all the nuances of communication. The simple truth is: if you don't like to write or speak to other people—find another job.

Effective Communications: An Enduring Challenge

As with most professional characteristics, any gaps in effective communication often start at the top—in our case, with the CAE. In chapter 2, I identified "effective communication skills" as one of the essential characteristics for today's internal auditors. In this section, I want to drive home that point by outlining the complaints I frequently hear about internal audit communication from stakeholders. Unfortunately, the following observations by audit committee members, managers, and others are far too common:

- Reports are too voluminous or not well-written.

- Committees receive too many reports or too much content.

- Audit results are "not synthesized" in a way that allows users to "connect the dots."

- Internal auditors are "introverts by nature" and reluctant to communicate informally.

- The CAE and senior internal audit staff don't give effective presentations.

- The CAE is reluctant to offer or issue opinions.

I could go on, but I suspect you get the point. As an internal audit professional, you should candidly assess your communication skills and continuously hone and develop them. Be confident in what you are communicating, whether it's spoken or written. Speak and write with conviction, passion, and authority. Be clear in what you say or write. Don't try to sound like someone else—be yourself—but articulate your thoughts so they are understood. Believe in what you are saying; your clients will quickly spot any hypocrisy. And don't talk at people—talk with them. Ask provocative questions and listen carefully to what they have to say.

LIFE LESSON #23

Effective internal auditors must do more than develop important information and insights. They must communicate that information and those insights effectively and continuously.

Closed Lips Are Missed Ships

During World War II, people were reminded of the dangers that enemy spies and submarines posed to wartime shipping with the phrase "loose lips sink ships." But when it comes to asking questions during an audit engagement, the danger is more often that "closed lips miss ships." Much of the information an internal auditor receives comes from interviews with managers and employees, and questions are the tool most commonly used to elicit that information. The reliability of that information depends in part upon how clearly the internal auditor is communicating with those being audited.

Be sure the questions you ask your clients are appropriate and designed to get you the information you need. Questions that elicit general or nonspecific responses are not productive and won't help you to identify any core problems. Open-ended questions will encourage the client to disclose all relevant information. Pay attention to what is *not* said and follow up when appropriate. Don't make assumptions based on incomplete information.

Regardless of how specific and complete your interview questions are, they are useless if you do not listen to the answers you're given. Hearing the words isn't enough; that just means you're aware of the sounds the person is making. Listening means you're paying attention to what it is they're saying and making a sincere effort to understand the meaning and significance of their words. Once internal auditors begin asking questions, they must demonstrate an appreciation for the answers by remaining alert, undistracted, and attentive. Ways to accomplish this and convey your efforts to the person speaking include:

1. *Monitor your nonverbal behavior.* Maintain comfortable eye contact and assume a posture of involvement by facing the speaker and perhaps leaning in the person's direction.

2. *Listen for feelings as well as facts.* As people speak, they usually reveal emotions as well as information. The speaker's tone, choice of words, and apparent frame of mind can be just as important as the information provided.

3. *Learn to listen reflectively.* A good way to confirm whether you have been listening well is to summarize what the speaker just said and ask if you have understood correctly.

4. *Listen with an open mind.* Don't let preconceptions about the person or the topic you're asking about cloud your understanding of what's being said. If you have preconceived notions about people or their answers, you're likely to selectively focus your attention on only the information that supports your expectations. Other ideas may be filtered out.[3]

Keep in mind that sensitive issues—such as management's failure to manage strategic or operational risks, ethically questionable behaviors, even allegations of fraud—could arise at any time, in which case the CAE and relevant internal audit staff must possess highly developed oral and written communication skills to ensure the information is conveyed to all concerned stakeholders in a timely and appropriate fashion. The communication of sensitive issues is best handled through well-established channels of formal and informal communication with management and board members with whom the CAE and internal audit have strong relationships based on trust and credibility.[4]

Setting the Tone During an Entrance Conference

Another time when effective communication is vital is during an engagement's entrance conference. If you have been in internal auditing for a few years, you've probably seen this happen. You start your entrance conference and everything is going smoothly. You've prepared carefully for the meeting and have cordial relationships with your audit clients. Suddenly, your clients are frowning and the communication seems to have become a one-way street. It's almost as if someone flipped a switch. Management's arms are crossed in a defensive posture; they seem to disagree with everything you say.

What went wrong? You may never know. All you do know is that an opportunity to discuss the scope, timing, and objectives of an upcoming audit with the relevant clients in a nonconfrontational atmosphere has slipped away. There are ways to help ensure it doesn't happen again, however. Every situation is different, but here are a few things you should avoid saying at entrance conferences because they seem to raise some people's hackles.

"We are here to help you." It's always good to establish and maintain a cordial tone throughout an entrance conference, but sincerity is the key. Clichés such as this are often referred to as "the oldest fib in internal auditing." The second-oldest is management's response to the opening, "We're glad to have you." Your client might actually be happy to see you—or you might be as welcome as the last government auditor to review their personal income taxes. If that's the case, your cheerful opening comment might unexpectedly fall flat.

"We are here because your area ranked high on our risk assessment." Any suggestion at an entrance conference that internal audit has already decided that problems exist will usually spark tension with management. You are undertaking this audit to assess the effectiveness of management's controls and risk management—if you think about the engagement from management's point of view, you can probably come up with a more compelling explanation for the audit.

"Our objective is to assess the overall effectiveness of your area." It is important that you articulate possible audit objectives as clearly, specifically, and precisely as possible. Broad terms such as *efficiency* or *overall effectiveness* are difficult to assess in the absence of widely accepted criteria. And remarks about an operation's "overall effectiveness" can give already anxious managers the jitters—the implication is that you are on some sort of "witch hunt" from which the client cannot possibly emerge unscathed.

"We will brief you on the results at the conclusion of the audit." Communication must be continuous. Holding the results until the end of an audit will invariably frustrate management and reinforce the stereotype of internal auditors as snoops with a "gotcha" mentality. It's OK to let clients know that you may not talk with them again until the conclusion of your visit—but only if you also make it clear

that there will be no surprises at that meeting. An entrance confer-ence should soothe unnecessary fears, not create anxiety about prob-lems that may not exist.

"We don't have anything to tell you today. We just wanted to know if you had any questions." If you schedule a meeting at which you have nothing to say, you are not just missing an opportunity to build relationships, you are wasting management's time. An entrance conference should be about sharing information, and you should prepare in advance so you can introduce the team members and talk about how the audit came to be, its preliminary objectives, projected milestones, and what may be expected of management. If you don't have anything to tell your client, stay in your office.

An internal audit's entrance conference is more than just a chance to say hello. It's an opportunity to make a strong first impression, to establish or reinforce healthy working relationships, and to motivate clients to work with you toward a positive outcome. It can set the tone for the entire engagement. Unfortunately, an entrance confer-ence can also damage working relationships; too often, mistrust is created or other barriers erected simply because of a thoughtless remark or errant phrase.

Avoiding Communication Breakdowns

As a young internal auditor, I was never more frustrated than when I presented what I knew to be a great recommendation or idea to an audit client, only to be met with waves of skepticism and negativity. I knew my message was important, but at times it was a real chal-lenge to overcome the mistrust and fear seemingly engendered by the mere fact that the recommendation had come from an auditor.

I didn't understand why I sometimes had difficulty "selling" my recommendations until one particular exit meeting that was unusually frustrating. Almost every recommendation from inter-nal audit elicited skepticism from the client—until a more experi-enced internal auditor joined the conversation. My colleague went back over several of the recommendations I had presented just a few moments earlier, and suddenly they seemed completely reasonable to our client.

Why was the other auditor so much more persuasive? I believe the difference was that the senior auditor had built a solid working relationship with the client and had firmly established his credibility.

Even when internal audit recommendations are sound, younger or newer auditors may lack the credibility to make them stick. Sometimes the problem is simply a lack of internal audit experience, but many times the problem stems from the auditor's communication skills. The good news is that communicating your credibility—the trust you inspire in others through honest and fair dealings with them—is a skill you can actively work to improve.

Here are some tips that should help you avoid at least a few of the frustrating exit meetings that I faced early in my career:

1. Maintain your enthusiasm.

We all tend to view people who are enthusiastic and passionate about their work as more credible than those who are not. It's difficult for others to buy into our ideas if we are seen as ambivalent or negative.

Maintaining a positive tone is particularly important when critiquing others. It's not enough that we are enthused by the situation; we must also stoke our client's enthusiasm for the changes we recommend. It's easier to develop enthusiasm when we concentrate on solving problems, not on finding fault. The next time you are tempted to say, "You did it wrong," instead try saying, "Let's see if there's a better way to do this."

2. Demonstrate your concern.

If you demonstrate genuine concern for your audit clients and their areas of responsibility, you will be well on your way to establishing some credibility (and building relationships). Yes, delivering promised results is critical for personal credibility—but nothing is more critical than constructive communication while delivering those results. When you show genuine concern for your clients, you are helping convince them that your audit recommendations are in their best interests.

3. BE PROFESSIONAL.

It may not always seem fair, but we are judged not only by the quality of our ideas but on how we present them as well. If you tend to dress sloppily, use slang or profanity, keep a disorganized work area, show up late for meetings, or chew gum throughout an exit meeting, don't be surprised when some clients assume you are also sloppy with your work. Being organized and professional in dress, speech, and behavior helps ensure that your ideas are taken seriously.

4. COMMUNICATE CONTINUALLY, CANDIDLY, AND (ALMOST) COMPLETELY.

Ongoing communication throughout an engagement can solidify your reputation as someone who is open to discussion even when those involved may not agree. Visibility is also critical: if co-workers and clients can't remember your name or face, you cannot establish any credibility.

I'm not suggesting that you monopolize meetings or bombard people with huge amounts of minute detail; I also don't mean to imply that discretion isn't important. Auditors often deal with sensitive information, and nothing can destroy someone's credibility faster than gossip or some other failure to preserve a client's confidentiality. Conversely, internal auditors must be particularly careful about agreeing to remain quiet about a potentially bad situation. You can't be credible as an internal auditor if you agree to hide anything immoral or illegal—it might even cost you your career.

5. FOLLOW THROUGH ON COMMITMENTS.

A reputation for dependability is essential in establishing your credibility, and following through on your tasks and promises shows your clients and co-workers that you are trustworthy and reliable.

Communication is essential if you realize you are going to miss a deadline or a commitment. But even if you apprise all relevant parties of the pending delay, too many excuses will damage your credibility further; perhaps the dog really did eat your audit report, but that doesn't change the fact that the report was not delivered when promised. It's important that you don't make promises unless you are sure you can keep them.

6. BE PREPARED.

If you arrive unprepared for meetings or don't know what you are talking about, you will lack credibility no matter what else you bring to the table. Preparation is especially important for auditors because each audit takes us into a new working situation. Asking questions is a key communication skill and can help build credibility, but it's important you do your homework first so that you don't ask unnecessary questions.

If you have not prepared for an audit ahead of time by learning about the industry and reading the files of previous audits, you are both destroying your credibility and wasting management's time.

7. GET IT RIGHT!

As Nathaniel Hawthorne said, "Accuracy is the twin brother of honesty; inaccuracy, of dishonesty." Whether an inaccuracy is a careless mistake, a deliberate exaggeration, or a downright lie, an internal auditor with a reputation for errors is always going to have credibility problems. If you're not sure of your facts—check them. If you're not sure about your audit procedures—get a second opinion.

Building credibility through effective communication takes time, but a solid reputation for honesty and fairness can follow you for the rest of your career—so for internal auditors, it is well worth the effort.

Continuous Communication— A Conduit for Information

I would be remiss if I concluded a discussion about continuous communication without reinforcing how vital this competency is to your career. As the CEO of The IIA, I have an extensive portfolio of stakeholders that includes more than 180,000 members, leaders in more than 100 affiliated international institutes and 150 chapters, the thirty-eight members of The IIA Global Board of Directors, and that board's Executive Committee. Communicating frequently with such a diverse and dispersed set of stakeholders is both challenging and necessary.

During the five years I have served as The IIA's chief executive, I have used the lessons I learned as a practicing internal auditor when communicating with The IIA's stakeholders. As CEO, I routinely communicate with stakeholders to:

- Learn their needs and expectations
- Understand the key metrics by which they will judge the organization's success
- Identify and mitigate key risks faced by the organization and profession
- Share news about key opportunities and accomplishments, as well as my assessment of organizational and industry risks
- Serve as a conduit for information from one key stakeholder group to another

During the many years I spent working as an internal auditor and leading internal audit departments, I never envisioned that I might someday be a CEO. But now that I am, I know I am a more effective CEO because of my experiences in internal auditing.

CHAPTER 9

Planning, the Most Important Phase of an Engagement

When I first joined the U.S. Postal Service (USPS) as deputy assistant inspector general for audit, I included among my responsibilities the task of reviewing all draft audit reports generated by the engagement teams. This was a frustrating process for everyone in the early going. The teams brought me their draft reports, proud of all the information they had collected and analyzed, but as I reviewed each of them ahead of their release to USPS management for comment, a common set of problems often emerged.

The audit's purpose and objectives were not clear in many of the draft reports, and both the scope of the audit and the methodology employed to conduct it were not well-defined. Initially, I assumed the audit teams were simply struggling with how to tell their story, but I soon discovered that the root cause of the confusion went all the way back to the planning phase of the audit's engagement.

On more than one occasion, a disillusioned team had to retroactively craft a plan to serve as the basis for the audit. In some cases, the team then had to return to the field to gather additional evidence, make extensive revisions to the report—which inevitably was delayed, diminishing its value to management accordingly.

Poor engagement planning is the first, and perhaps the biggest, mistake that internal auditors make in conducting and reporting their audits.

Timeliness in the Digital Age

Little more than a decade into the twenty-first century, we find ourselves in a digital age, with information moving instantaneously not only through mass media but through personal computers and various consumer devices, such as smartphones and tablets.

With the advent of digital text, images, and video, the speed and accessibility of information now defies imagination. I rarely find myself reaching for a TV remote anymore to find out on CNN or some other cable television outlet what is happening in the world. Instead, I log on to the Internet to scan news sites, check my email, or engage others on a social network. This world of instant news and information is where internal audit's clients and stakeholders live on a daily basis. Many organizations have installed enterprise systems with computerized "dashboards" that place vast amounts of real-time information at company executives' fingertips.

Yet timeliness continues to be a challenge for internal auditors. When I joined the profession in 1975, very little time was dedicated to planning an audit engagement. We often used some kind of "canned" template for our plan, charging off to conduct the audit much like a motorist with an old road map in the glove compartment. Some internal audit teams actually conducted internal audits without a plan at all, crafting one at the end of the process for filing with the rest of the engagement's work papers.

As anybody knows who has tried to navigate a trip along a new route with an outdated map or no map at all, it is easy to make wrong turns or become lost entirely. The same is true of an internal audit—if you don't have a sound, up-to-date plan, the engagement can easily go awry.

Careful planning at the outset of an engagement can eliminate many of the timeliness issues that internal auditors encounter during the actual engagement and reporting stages of their work.

An Expectations Gap

The internal audit profession has not made speeding up stakeholders' access to information much of a priority. The typical audit process today is much as it was forty years ago, before the introduction of mass-market personal computers. We use automation more than we did then, but it can still take an internal audit department two months or more to get an audit report to management.

Meanwhile, managers and the board of directors—our customers—live in the "Google era," with instant answers available to almost any question with a few keystrokes, and so they no longer consider two months, or even two weeks, very timely. This has created an *expectations gap* that is not often discussed in internal auditing.

Look at how the profession divides its energies and you'll see that an illustration of what internal auditors typically emphasize resembles an inverted pyramid. At the top is a large, wide band that represents accuracy; historically, we spend an incredible amount of time and resources to ensure the accuracy of our information, as well we should. Below that is a smaller band that represents usefulness; we spend a little less time focused on the degree to which our clients can use our information. And below that, the little triangle at the bottom represents the time we spend on our information's timeliness.

"Sometimes," George Bernard Shaw is reported to have quipped, "it's better never than late."

Management often needs to make urgent decisions. If they come upon a real or suspected problem, they might ask internal audit in to assess the situation or provide some assurance that the situation is under control, or they could be faced with a high-profile problem. I certainly encountered many of those during my years in government, particularly as an inspector general, when the morning newspaper might disclose a risk or problem that required me to deploy an audit team to quickly get to the bottom of it.

Deadlines imposed from outside the department can also be a problem. The CEO may ask the CAE to conduct an audit within a specific time frame, which is to say, "I need the answer within a week!" Health or safety concerns sometimes drive the need for quick turn-around of internal audit results.

And then there is the simple need to become more efficient. The faster we can wrap up an audit and distribute a report, the sooner we can move on to the next one, and the more audits we can produce in a year. That means more risks will be addressed each year. The challenge of balancing audit *quality* and *timeliness* has been around for a long time—I've faced it on and off for the past forty years. While the digital age has radically accelerated the flow of information, I haven't seen a whole lot of change within our profession.

The Planning Phase

Improving the timeliness of internal audits should start with the gap that now exists between what the profession continues to do and what its stakeholders have quickly come to expect. Each phase of the engagement process, starting with the planning stage, can then be reengineered to ensure that audit reports are not only accurate and reliable but timely as well.

The IIA's *Standards for the Professional Practice of Internal Auditing* (*Standards*) mandates that internal auditors undertake a "preliminary assessment of risks" at the outset of every engagement, then use the results of that risk assessment to build the audit program. Yet only about half of the internal audit engagements I have reviewed during the past decade included evidence of such a risk assessment.

Important Considerations During the Planning Phase

The planning phase should be where internal audit teams typically spend most of their time and resources. Yet many teams—impatient to arrive on site, roll up their sleeves, and conduct the actual audit— make only a half-hearted effort to document a plan before diving in. Here's what I suggest to internal auditors who work with me on an engagement:

Establish the objectives.

The first step in an internal audit engagement is to "conduct a preliminary assessment of risks relevant to the activity under review."[1] The engagement objectives must then reflect the results of the assessment. Assuming that management has already assessed risks in the area to be audited, consideration of management's assessment of risks is often the best place to start. In that regard, the internal auditor should consider:

- The reliability of management's risk assessment

- Management's process for monitoring, reporting, and resolving risk and control issues

- Management's reporting of events that exceeded the limits of the organization's risk appetite

- Risks in related activity to the activity under review[2]

Once the risk assessment has been completed, the engagement's formal objectives must be framed. To foster a timely audit, engagement objectives should be as precise as possible. In *Performance Auditing: A Measurement Approach*, Ronell Raaum and Steve Morgan offer some excellent advice on crafting precise objectives for performance audits. They recommend that to ensure objectives are precise as possible, they:

- Identify the audit subject
- Identify the performance aspects to be included
- Identify the finding and reporting elements the auditors expect to develop
- Be answerable[3]

Regardless of whether an internal audit is a performance audit or designed to pursue other objectives, I almost always advise internal auditors to pose them as questions that should be answered by the audit. For example: *"Do departmental contracting procedures conform to corporate contracting policies?"*

All other things being equal, there usually is a linear relationship between the number of questions we try to answer and how long it will take to conduct the audit. But audit timeliness can be affected by objectives that are framed too broadly, or as open-ended questions, which can become "black holes" swallowing time and resources. For example, an objective *"to assess the overall effectiveness of departmental contracting procedures"* is likely to take a long time to pursue should the criteria for "effectiveness" be too broad or ill-defined. Also, management might take strong exception if we were to conclude that the contracting procedures were "not effective" based on criteria that we developed. And such disagreements would further delay the final audit results.

Too many engagement objectives can actually be a bigger problem than having too few. That's because a large number of objectives may:

- Add time to the survey and planning phases of an audit

- Increase the scope of the engagement—expanding how much we have to look at and how much of it has to be documented

- Generate an overly complex audit plan, because each objective will need to be fleshed out in terms of specifying the procedures for identifying, analyzing, evaluating, and documenting information during the engagement

- Increase the size and elevate the expertise of the team needed to complete the assignment

- Increase the time required for doing fieldwork

- Increase the quantity of work papers eventually needed to document the audit's results

- Increase the complexity and size of the report

Based on my experience, limiting the number of objectives is one of the best ways to complete an audit in a timely manner. In deciding how to limit the number of objectives, the first step is to prioritize objectives based on the engagement risk assessment results discussed earlier. If I only have 200 staff hours or four calendar weeks to complete the engagement, then I want to ensure that the most significant risks are addressed with the resources or time constraints available.

Next, internal auditors should ask themselves a few questions about those who will use the information that the internal audit will likely generate:

- Is it going to be used by management?

- Is it going to be used by a board of directors?

- How quickly will the information be needed?

- Who is going to rely on it?

- What information are they seeking or do they need?

When framing objectives, I often advise internal auditors to think about what they already know. The traditional elements of an audit finding are *condition, criteria, cause and effect, and recommendations.* There are times when management will readily concede a condition and sometimes readily concede the cause and effect. When crafting an audit's objectives, there is no point in spending a lot of time documenting a point that management or those being audited concede at the outset. In such cases, it may be more prudent to frame that objective so it asks, *"Why* did the operating department exceed its budget by $1 million in the preceding year?"

INCREMENTAL AUDITING

One way internal auditors can ensure that their results are delivered in a timely fashion is through a technique I call *incremental auditing.* Incremental auditing involves taking an inventory of your audit's risk-based objectives and dividing them into a series of smaller engagements. If you have five objectives, you could decide to address the two objectives related to the biggest risk or the urgency that your stakeholders need the information in one audit, the two related to the next-biggest risk in a second audit, and the remaining one in a third audit. I have seen this approach work well in circumstances such as an audit designed to assess the response to a natural disaster.

Whether or not you use incremental auditing, there are times when it is critical that information from an audit report gets to management as soon as possible. That is when interim reports can be useful. The IIA's Practice Advisory 2410-1: Communication Criteria states that an interim report "[c]an be used to communicate information that requires immediate attention, to communicate a change in engagement scope for the activity under review, or to keep management informed of engagement progress when engagements extend over a long period."[4]

FRAME THE SCOPE OF THE AUDIT

Once the objectives have been established, the scope of the engagement must be determined. Since an engagement will rarely cover everything that can be audited related to the objectives, scope statements must be specific about what is and is not included within the engagement. Such statements may include:

Boundaries of the process—Defines at what point in the process the engagement will begin and where it will end.

In-scope versus out-of-scope locations—For processes that cover multiple locations, perhaps only some of those locations can or will be included in the engagement.

Subprocesses—Larger processes may be composed of a series of subprocesses.

Components—Certain portions, or components, of a process may be omitted.

Time frame—States the specific period of time covered by the engagement.

In addition to limiting your objectives, it is important to limit the scope of the engagement, because the scope also affects timeliness. If the scope is too broad or unrelated to the objectives, it will take more time to complete the audit. I've seen engagements that included an objective to provide assurance on a certain aspect of operations in the current year, yet the engagement team decided the scope of the audit would look at three years' worth of operational data.

Ideally, your objectives should yield self-evident time periods. So if a move is made to further limit a scope aligned with the audit's objectives, you may need to refine your objectives. Also, guard against "scope creep" during an audit engagement. If you find something interesting while testing records or results, don't expand your testing beyond the period for which you are trying to provide assurance without first seriously considering your reasons or the consequences. Obviously, if fraud is suspected or detected, expand the scope as needed.

Allocate Resources

Another way I have sped up the planning phase of an engagement is by engaging "functional experts" to assist the team in navigating the learning curve that invariably comes with planning the audit of a particular area for the first time.

I have found that bringing in people with expertise in the area you are auditing, at least during the planning phase, will help you shorten the learning curve. Sometimes it is essential that you get such help, especially if you're studying a highly technical area in which you lack expertise.

Generating internal audit results in a timely manner is much easier if you or someone on the team is knowledgeable about the area you are studying. Practice Advisory 2230-1: Engagement Resource Allocation notes that consideration should be given to the availability of external resources where additional knowledge and competencies are required.

You could hire these functional experts as permanent members of your staff, though that is often not practical. For example, at the Postal Service, we hired some engineers because of the vast complexities of the agency's real estate. You can contract with such specialists, which is probably the more common approach. It may also be possible to borrow such people from within your organization, though that can raise objectivity issues, so I would urge caution.

Develop the Engagement Work Program

Standard 2240: Engagement Work Program talks about the need to develop work programs that will enable achievement of the internal audit's objectives. These work programs can become very detailed and cumbersome—further undermining an audit's timeliness.

The form and the content of these work programs will vary depending on the area you are studying and the complexity of the audit plan for that area. The engagement program needs to include:

- The objectives of the engagement

- The technical requirements, processes, and transactions that are to be examined or tested

- The nature and extent of testing that will be required

- The procedures for collecting, analyzing, interpreting, and documenting information during the engagement[5]

Effective planning is the key to the successful completion of any type of project—especially that of the internal audit engagement. Remember that *failing to plan means planning to fail.* As discussed in chapter 8, communication takes place throughout the engagement process, as the team touches base with the audit's client about important matters on an interim basis—not just at the end of the process in the final engagement communication.[6]

An engagement's planning phase is the first and perhaps most important step in conducting a successful internal audit. Without adequate planning, the chances of missing relevant control weaknesses or encountering engagement-related problems increase considerably. Equally important, ineffective or inadequate planning can easily set you on the wrong path, undermining the timeliness of your work before you have even started.

CHAPTER 10

Fight the Temptation
to Over-Audit

Shortly after assuming the role of CAE for the first time in my career, I noticed that individual internal audits in my department were taking an unusually long time to complete. A closer look revealed that my internal audit teams were spending an inordinate amount of time preparing the work papers for each engagement—and I soon learned there was informal competition among the department's auditors to see who could generate the most voluminous work papers. I joked that the only thing missing was a copy of the phone book—but then I found one among one audit's set of work papers!

A small investigation on my part revealed what was fueling the competition. Back in the day, the internal auditors' names were displayed on the filing-cabinet drawers that held their work papers; this made it easy for them to monitor each other and measure who had the most work papers. Team members equated the sheer size of their paperwork with their relative proficiency as internal auditors. While an extreme example, the competition was fostered by an internal audit culture that rewarded comprehensiveness and accuracy at the expense of almost everything else. As the old saying goes, *what gets measured gets done.*

LIFE LESSON #25

Learn to avoid the instinctual tendency among internal auditors to over-audit and create unnecessarily voluminous work papers or electronic data.

From the outset of my career, it has been my experience that most internal auditors tend to over-audit. Blame it on the highly risk-averse nature of our profession. Being accurate and reliable is so ingrained in us early on that we end up auditing and documenting more than we really need to. The IIA's *Standards* is not overly prescriptive in terms of the methodology that must be deployed during internal audit engagements and does not mandate that work papers contain specific things. However, the policies of many internal audit departments, as well as other audit standards, are often very prescriptive. For example, Generally Accepted Government Auditing Standards (also known as the Yellow Book) includes almost forty pages of standards prescribing how fieldwork should be conducted for performance audits. Fourteen of those forty pages are dedicated solely to prescribing how sufficient and appropriate evidence is to be obtained and how audit evidence is to be documented.

Laboring under the pressure to ensure accuracy above all else, it is no wonder that internal auditors spend so much time on the *fieldwork* phase of their engagements. Whether you call the actual conducting of the audit *fieldwork* or simply talk about *performing the engagement*, as the *Standards* does, you are actually gathering, collecting, and analyzing evidence based on the audit's objectives so that you can draw basic conclusions that ultimately will be documented in your audit report.

While there is no magic formula for reducing the amount of time spent on an engagement, I'd like to share with you several strategies I've identified during my career that may help your internal audit department reduce its overall engagement cycle time.

Audit Techniques

To talk about performing the engagement is to talk about the techniques the internal audit team uses during its fieldwork. IIA Standard 2300: Performing the Engagement states, "Internal auditors must develop and document work programs that achieve the engagement's objectives."[1] The techniques employed should yield sufficient and competent evidence and ensure that the engagement is swift, yet done with due professional care.

Selecting the appropriate techniques can directly affect how long it takes to produce results. From my experience, certain techniques can improve the timeliness of internal audits, especially these:

Sampling

Historically, sampling has been a very effective time-saving tool. Before technology made it easier to gather and evaluate larger pools of data, sampling allowed us to limit the number of actions an auditor had to perform, or the number of documents that had to be collected, or the number of locations that had to be visited, without materially affecting the results. Sampling allowed us to draw conclusions about transactions or balances without spending the time and money to examine every transaction. Sampling is still used when it isn't efficient to review 100 percent of the available records, which is often the case if only hard-copy versions of the records are maintained. Sampling is also useful if inventories of physical assets are necessary. And sampling may be used if records are in remote locations or other circumstances make reviewing all of them by electronic means difficult.

Flowcharting and Process Mapping

Flowcharting processes and activities allow you to quickly evaluate all the steps that occur during an activity or function in a department for which you are conducting an audit.

Flowcharts, by the way, can add stakeholder value to an audit. I've had clients who were more excited about the flowcharts that we developed and included in our work papers than they were about the final audit report. Some even posted copies on the walls above their desks.

Flowcharts are a great tool to visualize complex systems inside an organization, and often they are easier to understand and less time-consuming for others than a narrative would be. Flowcharts enable both the auditor and the client to quickly grasp the big picture. And in the current age of digital technology, it is relatively easy to create a flowchart. It is also easier to update the information in a flowchart than it would be to rewrite a narrative description of the process being audited.

Regression Analysis

Regression analysis helps you identify anomalies using advanced analytical techniques and then, based on an analysis of those anomalies, tells you where you need to focus your efforts. That can save you time and money.

It can also be very useful during the planning phase of an engagement, when you are trying to determine the objectives and scope of the audit. *Sawyer's Guide for Internal Auditors* defines regression analysis as a "[s]tatistical technique used to establish the relationship of a dependent variable to one or more independent variables. For example, an internal auditor might estimate payroll expense based on the number of employees, average rate of pay, and the number of hours worked, and then compare the result to the recorded payroll expense."[2]

Thanks to the availability of modern, off-the-shelf software such as Microsoft Excel, tools like regression analysis are easy for internal auditors to use.

Collecting and Documenting Audit Data and Evidence

An important element of the audit engagement is the collection of evidence to be used in evaluating, preparing, and communicating the audit results to your client. There are several types of audit evidence that can serve as a basis for conclusions.

TESTIMONIAL EVIDENCE

Testimonial evidence is what people say to the auditor. It is considered the weakest form of evidence, though certain testimonial evidence is stronger than others. For example, the person who performs a task could provide stronger evidence of how that task is actually performed than could a supervisor who may know only how it *should* be performed.

As a general rule, people who are independent of—but knowledgeable about—the activities being reviewed will provide more reliable testimonial evidence than will the people who are actually involved in the activities.

When documenting testimonial evidence, try to avoid long, detailed transcripts of your interviews, unless they reveal significant anomalies such as material waste, mismanagement, or fraud. Instead, I have coached my auditors to summarize the interviews—particularly if they are corroborated by other types of evidence.

DOCUMENTARY EVIDENCE

Documentary evidence is contained in some sort of a permanent record form, such as a hard-copy version of an audit report or a supplemental IT system digital archive. This is the second strongest type of evidence, though it may not be as strong as it appears. It is important to consider the source of the document. A written memo is not much stronger than testimonial evidence, for example, because it proves the person said what is in the memo but does not prove that what is said is true.

Documents from sources external to the organization are much stronger evidence than internal documents. External documents from external sources sent to the organization are usually stronger than internal documents, though they are not as strong as those sent directly to the internal auditors.

In working with internal audit teams, I have always advised them that it is not necessary to include paper or electronic copies of every document examined in the audit's work papers. In my experience, much of that documentary evidence amounts to what I call "happy work papers."

Happy work papers are simply evidence that everything is fine—that observed conditions conform to criteria. Such documentation does not need to be included in its entirety, though the work papers should note what was observed and include notations that would enable an experienced internal auditor to retrieve the same documentation and draw the same conclusions. Documentary evidence indicating conditions that do not conform to criteria should be included in the work papers—particularly if fraud is involved. This type of documentation has a tendency to "grow legs and walk away" after the audit is completed, if management elects to dispute the audit results or if someone is accused of wrongdoing.

PHYSICAL EVIDENCE

Physical evidence is evidence the auditors see with their own eyes. This is considered the strongest form of evidence, though it is important for the auditor to consider what the evidence proves and what it does not prove.

With the advent of the digital age, it is very easy for internal auditors to capture images of physical evidence. During my tenure at the Postal Service in the late 1990s, the inspector general's office documented safety and environmental conditions at an older postal facility using video technology. With the advent of smartphones and other digital technology, documenting physical evidence in the field is even easier and faster.

ANALYTICAL EVIDENCE

Analytical evidence is obtained by comparing, computing, or otherwise analyzing data. Analytical evidence—assuming the data analyzed is accurate—proves that certain relationships exist among the data. This usually has to be investigated further to determine why the relationships exist.

IIA Standard 2310: Identifying Information states that "[i]nternal auditors must identify sufficient, reliable, relevant, and useful information to achieve the engagement's objectives." It interprets each of these criteria as follows:

> *Sufficient* information is factual, adequate, and convincing so that a prudent informed person would reach the same conclusions as the auditor.
>
> *Reliable* information is the best attainable information through the use of appropriate engagement techniques.
>
> *Relevant* information supports engagement observations and recommendations and is consistent with the objectives for the engagement.
>
> *Useful* information helps the organization meet its goals.[3]

One way to improve the timeliness of an audit is to shorten the process in the way you gather your evidence. Avoid over-auditing by taking care to document your findings with the strongest type of evidence, which then makes it unnecessary to gather weaker evidence for the same findings. If gathering the stronger evidence would be too time-consuming, you may be able to accomplish the same thing by quickly gathering several weaker types of evidence that corroborate each other. And remember: it is not necessary to include all of these types of evidence in every set of your internal audit's work papers.

Work Paper Contents and Preparation

I am probably more liberal than many of my peers when it comes to documentation and work paper preparation. I always remind myself that work papers are a means and not an end. By that I mean that work papers are an important element of the audit's system of quality controls, so they must be comprehensive enough to form the basis of any conclusions we reach and communicate to our clients, but those clients rarely see them.

Although I am sometimes critical of the prescriptive nature of the Yellow Book, I believe that its discussion in Paragraph 6.79, "Audit Documentation," conveys the right message about the contents of work papers:

> "Auditors must prepare audit documentation related to planning, conducting, and reporting for each audit. Auditors should prepare audit documentation in sufficient detail to enable an experienced auditor, having no previous connection to the audit, to understand from the audit documentation the nature, timing, extent, and results of audit procedures performed, the audit evidence obtained and its source and the conclusions reached, including evidence that supports the auditors' significant judgments and conclusions. An experienced auditor means an individual (whether internal or external to the audit organization) who possesses the competencies and skills that would have enabled him or her to conduct the performance audit. These competencies and skills include an understanding of (1) the performance audit processes, (2) GAGAS and applicable legal and regulatory requirements, (3) the subject matter associated with achieving the audit objectives, and (4) issues related to the audited entity's environment."[4]

Automated Audit Management Systems

There's no doubt that audit management systems, with their electronic work paper components, are the greatest development yet for those determined to streamline the audit process. Although electronic work papers were an emerging technology ten years ago, they are widely used today. Unfortunately, however, quite a few internal auditors still resist using them.

True, learning to use electronic work papers requires a period of adjustment during which it may actually take you longer to document an audit than if you had stuck with your conventional audit documentation methodologies. That's why it is important to remember that automated audit management is a *system*, not just a place in which to store your audit documentation. Automated work paper systems can handle management and administrative tasks considerably faster and more easily than the older, manual systems can.

In the days before automated work papers, it was unusual to find an internal audit department that regularly tracked its findings and open issues. The administrative burden of tracking scores of open issues was often daunting. Yet, with no way to easily monitor whether management took action on the department's recommendations, important risks were sometimes overlooked or ignored. Today, automated work paper systems streamline administrative tasks such as follow-up tracking and the scheduling of audits. They also speed the sharing of information and work paper reviews. Automated work papers also add consistency to a department's audits, which can help with quality control and further eliminate the reworking of reports and other documents.

ELECTRONIC WORK PAPERS

With the introduction of personal computers in the early 1990s, internal auditors began to discuss the benefits of automating the historical work paper process. The hard-copy process was cumbersome and had changed little since the beginning of the century. One of its major drawbacks: you had to be present to examine the material. Using electronic work papers, several people could pull up the same file on their computers from different locations and discuss the findings. But safeguards were needed—tools to generate an audit trail as auditors added notations, wrote off items with check marks, and inserted links to specific tests and findings.

Mike Gowell, a former PwC colleague and now general manager and vice president of TeamMate in Tampa, Florida, was involved in creating the first electronic work paper audit software. Research he initiated showed that internal auditors spent 33 percent of their time documenting their efforts in work papers—and only 28 percent of their time auditing. Electronic work papers obviate the need for hard-copy storage and add functionality to the online file, allowing for things like the easy insertion of additional documents that weren't part of the original work paper.

AUDIT SCHEDULING

As discussed in chapter 9, the CAE is responsible for ensuring a schedule is developed each year that lists the areas within the organization to be audited. The annual audit plan typically includes a designation as to which members of the internal audit team are assigned to each planned engagement. Assigning the right people with the right skills to each audit is vital to managing the internal audit function.

Electronic scheduling tools make this job faster and easier to do. Once the CAE has entered profiles of each auditor into the system—showing languages spoken, specialty skills, areas of expertise (such as purchases and inventory, or vendor management), and the like—the scheduling system can quickly match the right auditor to each audit. The process is integrated into the audit management system, so the team's scheduler can automatically schedule each audit and auditor in the electronic work papers.

DATA ANALYTICS, DATA MINING, DATA REQUISITION

Areas where electronic auditing tools are still evolving include data analytics, data mining, and data requisition. Such systems allow auditors to access 100 percent of the information for testing in areas of concern, such as duplicate payments to vendors. In the past, information could only be sampled. Thanks to data analytics, an auditor can ask IT to generate a list of every check cut the previous year grouped by vendor.

Data analytics uses IT files and IT interrogations to do audit testing. It allows for continuous controls monitoring. Reports can be run automatically every night, if necessary.

These systems have quickly become fundamental tools of internal auditing; they can greatly improve a department's efficiency and effectiveness, and the quality of its work. An internal auditor or audit department that is not using these systems is simply not going to produce audits as effective or timely as they could be.

Closing the Effectiveness Gap

Internal audit departments are constantly being offered new technology designed to improve their work. (You will read about more of them in chapter 12.) But these new electronic systems are of no value unless CAEs have at least a rudimentary understanding of how to use them and require their staffs to incorporate the technology into every audit they complete.

When CAEs were recently asked to rate the importance of effectively leveraging technology to benefit their organization, 70 percent to 80 percent said it's "very important" to "extremely important." But when these same CAEs were asked to rate themselves on how effectively they were leveraging technology within their department, only 20 percent said they were doing well. That's quite an effectiveness gap.[5]

Presumably, all of these CAEs want to close this gap; they realize the importance of leveraging the technology. According to The IIA's Audit Executive Center, five key strategies can help make that happen:

1. *Set the tone at the top.* If the CAE doesn't make an effort to embrace the technology and doesn't make it a strategic priority, the internal auditors aren't likely to either. The CAE has to articulate the benefits of such technology to the staff and require that it become a priority

for every audit. The CAE must also budget resources for training.

2. *Make electronic tools mandatory for every audit.* Unless you start by making it compulsory, the gap will linger.

3. *Invest in training.* In the survey mentioned earlier, CAEs were asked how they trained their teams in the use of new technology, and how proficient their teams were in using it. Did they bring in an outside instructor? Organize formal instruction and classes led by someone in the department? Or settle for on-the-job training? The correlation between type of training and staff proficiency couldn't have been any more obvious: those departments that chose on-the-job training had the lowest rates of proficiency among their staffs. On-the-job training doesn't seem to always cut it where use of technology is concerned.

4. *Hire someone with technology skills.* Not every internal auditor will become an expert user of the latest technological tools. Some CAEs are finding it hard to transform just any auditor into a data analytics expert. Instead, they are hiring an IT expert and making that person the internal audit department's technology champion. An added benefit of this arrangement: having such an expert within the department ensures that internal audit will not miss out or be slow to learn about emerging technologies. Teams that budget money for training and hire a technology champion seem to have shorter learning curves.

5. *Measure what matters.* Have metrics in place to measure the return on investment from your new technology and to show others you are not licensing technology and then failing to use it effectively. If you can show the audit committee or CEO a return on the organization's

investment, they will be more inclined to support your technology initiative.

The Interview Process

No discussion on streamlining field work would be complete without addressing the processes by which interviews are conducted. During an engagement, internal auditors derive a significant amount of their information about the operations under study, as well as related control activities and deficiencies, from interviews with other people. As I discussed in an earlier chapter, active listening is as important to an internal auditor as the ability to solicit, verify, compare, and evaluate information. Important techniques for effective listening include making eye contact with speakers during individual and group encounters, expressing your interest through questions, restating what someone has said to ensure clarity, avoiding unnecessary interruptions, looking for subtle meanings and feelings that may not be overtly expressed, and responding appropriately to what you have heard.[6]

I once spoke with an auditor who had just spent the previous week combing through contract provisions, painstakingly gathering supporting documents for what he thought would be an important finding—only to discover that the contract provisions were no longer in force. If he had asked a few more questions at the beginning of the week, he would have discovered that, because of a series of change orders, many of the provisions in the original contract were no longer valid. The audit was still a success because at the end of the week—and well before the closing meeting—he asked his client to explain what appeared to be numerous discrepancies. But who knows what else might have been accomplished during that week of lost productivity.

DEVELOP EFFECTIVE INTERVIEWING SKILLS

For many years, I taught accounting during evening courses at a local university. I would often tell my students, "The only stupid question is the one that is never asked—unless the question is, 'Would you postpone the next exam?'"

My years as a college instructor coincided with the early years of my career in internal auditing, my day job at the time. And so I came to appreciate that in internal auditing, as elsewhere in life, there really are very few stupid questions.

LIFE LESSON #26

A successful internal auditor understands that the biggest risk during an audit is not citing a finding that doesn't exist—it's overlooking a finding that does exist.

The most successful internal auditors are not necessarily the smartest or the most experienced; often, they are simply the most inquisitive. Of course, it also helps to be intelligent and well-prepared for what's to come, but when internal auditors miss a finding, too often it's simply because they weren't curious enough to ask all the questions they should have.

Consider this: if you cite an issue or problem in your draft report that does not exist, management will usually object vehemently and provide ample evidence that your conclusions are erroneous (which is why I often cite management review of a draft report as one of the best forms of quality control during an audit). But if you fail to cite an issue or problem that really does exist, how often does management speak up and say, "Excuse me, but you've missed a major deficiency in my area."? Let's just say that, in almost forty years on the job, I have never seen it happen.

We also need to be able to assess risks, plan engagements, conduct fieldwork, analyze situations, and advise our clients appropriately. But the overall process (and each step within it) starts with asking well-informed questions.

My colleague, Jodi Swauger, describes this as the "Five A's Formula for Success":

Audit Ability = Asking + Analyzing + Advising—in that order.

Is informed questioning really that important? Absolutely! The right questions can be the difference between nailing a powerful finding in just a few minutes and spending days on fieldwork that uncovers a problem everyone else already knew about—or, worse yet, overlooks a fresh problem completely.

It is important not to conduct interviews like interrogations. And remember that the client should do most of the talking, and you most of the listening.

Avoid Drive-By Auditing

Nothing undermines the value of an internal audit more than delivering the results once it's too late to correct a problem or prevent further fraud, waste, or mismanagement. But at the other extreme are what I call "drive-by" internal audits that rely on canned programs or checklists. These quickie audits are sometimes conducted at the branch or store level in the financial-services and retail industries.

Don't get me wrong—drive-by audits can provide important assurance on the effectiveness of internal controls and compliance matters. They can also help deter fraud. But their use does not always comply with our professional standards, and they rarely provide management with real value. I often think of these down-and-dirty engagements as "inspections" rather than true internal audits.

To avoid becoming a drive-by auditor, I recommend you assess your approach by asking yourself these five questions:

1. *Is the engagement the result of an annual or ongoing risk-assessment process?* Drive-by audits are often cyclical: "We are going to audit you this year whether you need it or not."

2. *Is the audit program or engagement plan based on an assessment of risk?* As noted earlier, the *Standards* mandates that, in planning an engagement, internal auditors must consider significant risks to the activity, its objectives, resources, and operations. Drive-by audits often use canned audit materials, with little consideration given to the risks facing the specific business unit or activity that is the focus of the engagement.

3. *Is the same audit program being used at each drive-by location?* As indicated above, an audit program should be tailored to the risks of the specific unit. But there is an even bigger problem with repeated use of the same program at multiple locations: management will quickly ascertain the areas subject to audit and prepare themselves for the auditor's arrival at subsequent locations. Even if a new audit program is used each year, I have seen instances where management from the first business unit audited as part of the annual cycle alerts their colleagues further down the schedule to "what the auditors are looking at this year." Naturally, that can undermine the effectiveness of the entire audit process.

4. *Does the final audit report offer recommendations or simply provide findings or observations?* Although it's rare, some drive-by internal auditors don't even attempt to develop customized recommendations for taking corrective action in response to the findings or noncompliance issues cited in their audit report. The final report is nothing more than a list of transgressions compiled by the auditor before heading off to the next location. Rather than a drive-by internal audit, this should be classified as a "hit-and-run" internal audit.

5. *Does the audit process and final report provide management with any added value?* Sadly, in the case of drive-by
audits, the answer is often "no." The reports are often
very clinical, with no indication of management's accomplishments, insight on operations, or opportunities for
improvement beyond the boilerplate "these things are
not in compliance—correct them."

Every phase of the internal audit process must be reengineered
with an eye toward producing more timely results. But while new,
digital tools for the planning and fieldwork stages, such as automated
work papers, have certainly streamlined internal auditors' work, the
most daunting part of the process in terms of timeliness is the reporting phase. In the next chapter, I will share with you the challenges I
have faced in the reporting phase, and how I learned to deliver timely,
effective reports.

CHAPTER 11

Internal Audit Reporting: The Ultimate Obstacle to Timeliness

It would be nice if a typical internal audit, well-planned in advance and employing the latest technology to speed up the fieldwork, was then destined for swift delivery to the audit's client. Unfortunately, crafting the actual internal audit report and obtaining management's concurrence with applicable findings and recommendations can be the most time-consuming—and frustrating—phase of all.

In his iconic book *Sawyer's Guide for Internal Auditors*, Larry Sawyer nails it when he describes the process of writing an audit report this way: "Few sources of friction within the auditing department exceed that caused by the process of report writing. The most brilliant of analyses and the most productive of audit findings seem to be forgotten during the trauma of report writing."[1]

Typical Challenges in the Reporting Process

As a young internal auditor, I was certainly frustrated now and then by the writing of internal audit reports. But I imagine it is much more frustrating for new auditors today.

The challenge to produce internal audit reports in a more timely manner, for clients now accustomed to instantaneous transmission of information in the digital age, competes with the other criteria for communicating audit results to clients—especially accuracy. The same hurdle exists in the planning and fieldwork phases of the internal audit process.

We are trained from the outset of our careers that we cannot afford to generate inaccurate internal audit reports. We also strive to craft reports that pass muster with management and result in improvements or corrective action within the organization. Combine these demands with a multilevel review process within the internal audit department, and writing an audit report can become an exercise in delay and frustration.

The first time new internal auditors send in a draft audit report for review, they may naively think the audit is finished as they shift gears mentally to begin focusing on the challenges and uncertainties of the next engagement. Little do they know that the reporting phase of that audit has just started.

It helps to know what to expect when a draft is sent up the departmental chain for review; that is, someone will look it over and indicate desired changes to your carefully chosen words—and trust me, if it is your first audit report, there *will* be changes. The draft will be sent back to you for revision, and when you're done with it, again, the new version will be sent back to the first reviewer, who may or may not forward it to the next level of review, depending on how pleased they are with your revisions.

If your internal audit department is large enough, a second reviewer might then take a more strategic view of how the report should be written, and they often append extensive comments. Back will come the report to your audit team, and once the questions are answered and additional revisions made, it will then be forwarded back up the chain through the first two levels of review.

At this point many audit groups require a process called *referencing*. Referencing is an accuracy check that involves cross-referencing every word in the report with a source document or other supporting evidence from the audit's work papers. This can take a surprising amount of time (particularly if you didn't heed the advice on work papers in chapter 10), after which the draft report will make its way back down through the same review channels for questions or comments about the cross-referencing results.

Next, if you are part of a really large internal audit department, a professional editor may review the draft report before it's issued. Many internal audit departments also send their drafts to the general counsel or legal department for review, particularly in government settings, where audit reports tend to generate newspaper headlines. At each point in the process, fresh comments, questions, and revisions may demand your attention.

Discouraged yet? Don't be; there's more to come. Until a few years ago, some internal audit reports were pulled from the files independently reviewed as a quality-assurance measure long after the conclusion of the engagement. But the quality-improvement programs at a growing number of organizations now require peer reviews of all audit work papers *before* a draft report is issued. So all work papers must be well crafted, too, because your report may resurface again with additional comments and questions.

Given the number of safeguards built into the report-review process, it's not surprising that it sometimes takes weeks or months to get a draft out the door—at which point that frustrated new auditor may learn, as I did early in my career, that an explosive reaction to the draft report from the audit client can trigger parts of the review process to start over again. You may find yourself immersed in a weeks-long process of negotiation involving numerous explanations and clarifications before the client accepts the findings.

The good news is that there are ways to sidestep many of the pitfalls in the audit-reporting process. And, if all else fails, there are some fundamental strategies that may help save some time.

Time-Saving Strategies

Often information in an internal audit report is urgent. But even when the findings or recommendations don't need immediate attention, speedier delivery of audit reports is becoming more essential as clients' expectations rise amid the ongoing explosion of information in the digital age. We all like to know where we stand when we're being examined. Imagine for a moment that you're still in college and your professor has just told the class he won't have your grades until four months after the final exam. Oh, sure, a few students might be pleased with the delay, but most of you will likely be grumbling in the hallways and perhaps even complaining to the dean!

Obviously your internal audit clients are not college students, but if an audit report is not out the door four months after the fieldwork is complete, you're likely to hear some grumbling around the water cooler. When people stop what they are doing at work to talk about the results of an internal audit, chances are good you are making a difference in your organization; but if they drop what they're doing to grouse about an audit report that they expected to see months ago, the difference you're making in the organization is not necessarily something to be proud of.

During the past decade, I have worked with quite a few audit departments that have taken on the challenge of audit reports' timeliness. Many of them have achieved enviable results in reducing their reports' "cycle time." Based on my observations, there are at least six strategies that, if deployed effectively, can substantially reduce the amount of time it takes to issue internal audit reports:

I. SHARE INTERNAL AUDIT RESULTS WITH CLIENTS "AS YOU GO."

Client "push back" against an audit report can be intensified by the shock effect of seeing all of the results at once. Providing the client with results incrementally can help. Once the internal audit team gets to the point in the engagement where they are satisfied there is a reportable condition, you should share the information with your client, either informally or through an interim audit memorandum. Regular communication with clients during the audit—including sharing draft findings and recommendations in writing—goes a long way toward fostering a positive reaction when the full report is presented for comment.

2. ELIMINATE OR REDUCE LEVELS OF REVIEW.

Multiple levels of review within the internal audit department are often a major source of delays in audit reporting. Streamlining the review process and reducing the number of reviewers can shorten and speed up the process.

Large organizations in particular seem to get quite a few people involved in crafting their engagement reports yet, in my experience, the reports produced for these organizations are not necessarily better than reports written elsewhere that undergo only one or two reviews. Many of the organizations I've worked with over the years have found that, if you eliminate some of the additional reviews, the reports move along much more quickly. Others have delegated the reviews to lower-level staff. Such tactics entail some risk; every additional review provides a fresh viewpoint and a different level or type of expertise, while having more-senior staff do reviews ensures more experienced eyes will examine the drafts. Sacrificing those could affect reports' accuracy, clarity, and constructiveness; for example, considerations that should be weighed when attempting to speed up the process. Reducing levels of review is a way to move the audit along faster, but it pays to consider the risks.

3. USE AN EDITOR EARLIER IN THE PROCESS.

Larger audit organizations such as national offices or U.S. federal IGs tend to have professional editors; and in my mind, the editor should have first crack at revising the draft report. As soon as a draft is available from the engagement team, the professional editor should take over. There is no point in having auditors higher up the ladder worry about correcting grammar and syntax; the time of these amateur editors is best spent focused on actual audit issues. Using the professional editor earlier in the process can move things along quickly.

4. USE TEAM WRITING TO CONDENSE THE PROCESS.

Bringing the audit team together with all of those who will edit or review the draft report for a single editing session can reduce reports' cycle time dramatically. This approach allows the internal audit team and the department's upper-level supervisors to discuss the draft report and propose changes without the endless back and forth of the usual editing process. This is a strategy I used when working for the USPS OIG in the late 1990s.

Team writing brings together the engagement team, the first- and second-level reviewers, the editor, the referencer, and the lawyers (if any are involved). Everyone sits around a table in a conference room, with the audit report projected onto a screen at the front of the room, and each person commits to not leaving that room until the review process is complete.

This is one of the fastest ways to reach consensus on a draft report, but it can actually be more costly in terms of total staff hours than conventional review processes. At the USPS, it generally took us about an hour per page to edit the draft, and each person there was committed to spending the entire time on the review. If we began with an eight-page draft report, it often took upwards of a day of each person's time to complete a team-writing review.

But when team editing is done correctly, once you're done, you are done. You don't have to worry about anyone circulating new versions of the report, and the draft report gets out the door much sooner.

Team editing is a powerful tool for shortening the report process and improving the timeliness of an organization's internal audits. The group dynamic also allows newer auditors to gain valuable insights about report writing from the team's more experienced members. I recall one instance at the Postal Service when we were able to deliver a fully coordinated draft audit report to management for comment only forty-eight hours after the fieldwork was complete!

5. REPORT CONFERENCING.

Report conferencing is a somewhat more daring version of team writing. Similar to team writing, because it brings all reviewers together in the room, report conferencing also brings your audit clients to the table—so the people you have audited can offer their two cents' worth before the draft report is issued.

It makes many internal auditors nervous to have their clients in the room while the audit report is being drafted or edited, and you do need to build in safeguards when using this approach. Obviously, the internal auditors have to retain control of the final product, but overcoming clients' objections is always part of the reporting process, and those I've talked with who have tried conferencing are generally positive about the approach. It certainly eliminates management's frustration with reports that don't show up for weeks or months, and when done successfully, it can cut the time between a draft and the final report to almost nothing.

6. STREAMLINE THE AUDIT REPORT.

Internal audit departments that have successfully reduced their reports' cycle time generally produce leaner audit reports, which makes them not only easy to edit but easy to read. The shorter a report is, the less time it typically takes to write and edit. Complexity can also slow the review process, so generally speaking, simpler is better, too. And reaching consensus with clients can become onerous with longer reports, so streamlining formats pay dividends throughout the process.

I have on occasion seen internal audit reports that exceeded one hundred pages. I am convinced reports that long are not read in their entirety by all of those who were likely to benefit from the information. It's always tempting to include more detail in an internal audit report than the minimum needed to make your point, but my advice to new auditors: tell your story clearly and succinctly. There's nothing worse than working hard and coming up with a good report that people then ignore. Think of it this way: the longer your report, the less likely it will be read by those in a position to take action on your recommendations.

Some internal audit departments model their reports on those issued by large accounting and consulting firms. At first glance, this seems logical: those firms have tried-and-true report formats that work extremely well for them. But our reports are usually not intended for public audiences, so it may not be necessary to include lengthy company descriptions, legal disclaimers, or minutely detailed descriptions of our methodologies in every report. I once saw an internal audit report about payroll processes, for example, that included the year the company was founded, its location, its motto, its vision statement, and descriptions of each of its major product lines—all before it said anything about payroll processing. When I asked why that information was included, I was told it was standard procedure to include it in every report issued by the department. Presumably, the company's audit committee had long ago learned to skip ahead when opening a report; one can only hope they didn't skip all the way to the back cover, though that is a danger whenever an audit report doesn't make every word count.

If your department is considering streamlined report formats, remember that electronic report formats allow you to embed hyperlinks in the copy that direct readers to additional information if they think they need it. A hyperlink might open a source document, for example, thus eliminating the need to spend much time describing that source information in your report. This can result in a concise report designed to meet the needs of different audiences by providing details only for those readers who seek them.

The Three-Inch Audit Report

Perhaps the most extreme example in my experience of streamlining a report and speeding up the reporting process occurred during my time as FORSCOM director of internal review. As fighting ended in the 1990–1991 Gulf War, I helped deploy a military internal audit team to the Mideast as part of Operation Desert Storm. Resources over there were limited, and everyone throughout the Army was operating under very constrained conditions, including those of us in internal review.

The commander at one military facility was a three-star general and a deputy of U.S. Army Gen. Norman Schwarzkopf, commander of the thirty-four-nation coalition that fought Iraq. Every morning, this three-star general met with all of his direct reports, including internal review. He told his deputies, all of the generals and colonels reporting to him, "If you have a problem, you come to me with it. But I am only going to take problems or challenges written on 3-by-5-inch index cards. I'll assign them out for solutions or corrective actions."

"But we have to give you our reports!" the internal auditors said. The general was unimpressed—managing such a complex military operation depended on responding rapidly to concise reports from every group in the room—internal reviews included. The auditors were limited to the same 3-by-5-inch index cards as everyone else.

With some effort and creativity, the internal auditors were able to condense their audit issues and recommendations so they each fit on a standard index card while meeting applicable audit standards. The general took the 3-by-5-inch cards and handed them out during his morning staff meetings to the appropriate individuals for corrective action.

Every organization is unique, and I assume you will never have a 3-by-5-inch limit imposed on your internal audit reports. But you do need to find innovative ways to produce those and improve their timeliness. And the strategies outlined above have worked in numerous organizations around the world.

Dealing with Push Back

The first time management takes strong exception to one of your draft audit reports is likely to be a significant and emotional event— for you as well as the client. You might be tempted to lash out or become intransigent, though neither of these options would serve you well.

Difficult, emotional client meetings are often best handled with the calm assistance of more seasoned members of the internal audit team. In all likelihood, your supervisor or the CAE have plenty of experience with contentious audit results and have likely built relationships with management that can mean the difference between success and failure, while helping to resolve the standoff as painlessly as possible. If you have not yet experienced such a situation, I strongly advise that, when it does happen to you (and sooner or later it *will* happen if you stay in internal audit long enough), you should immediately seek help from a more experienced auditor.

No matter how emotional a client might get, in my experience that client's objections to your report are often not as severe as they might first appear. You may discover that you concentrated so hard on "selling" your findings and recommendations that you forgot to deliver a *balanced message*. The problem may not be what you have written as much as what you didn't write; I frequently find that most of a client's frustrations can be relieved merely by adding a few sentences of context to a report that highlight accomplishments observed or look at the findings in terms of the organization's overall operations.

It is easy to fall into the trap of reporting only negative results. After all, finding problems is what they pay us for, right? But we shouldn't limit our assurance to what isn't working well, and when a draft report fails to indicate satisfactory performance as much as warranted, clients may conclude that we are not presenting an objective image of their operations.

I developed during my career a growing appreciation of the need to choose my words carefully. I came to understand that a well-written internal audit report, while a call to action, can result in inappropriate actions—or no action at all—because of a single poorly chosen word or phrase. I witnessed cases where poor report writing actually harmed an internal auditor's reputation or made it impossible to build or continue effective working relationships with others.

By the time I became a supervisor, I no longer considered my supervisors' editing of reports as unreasonable as they had once seemed. As a CAE, I found myself editing my team's audit reports as rigorously as my former supervisors had edited mine. I did try, however, to resist perpetuating the age-old tradition of changing "happy" to "glad."

Tone of the Report Is Important

Regardless of how well we communicate during engagements, our clients often remain sensitive or fearful about internal audit reports. You may be confident that your report is timely, accurate, and *perfectly crafted*, yet it still might be received with a resounding thud. Sometimes it can't be avoided, but with practice we can often keep that from happening. You've probably heard the old saying,

"It's not what you say, it's how you say it that counts." Well, in internal auditing, it's a combination of both. The content of our audit reports must always add value to the organization, but the way we communicate in our reports will determine how those findings and recommendations are received.

What we perceive as objective reporting can sometimes trigger fear or anger from those being audited. They may feel as though their integrity or judgment is being attacked; they may also be reading the report while thinking, "How will my bosses react when they read this?" Even if they do not view a report as needlessly critical, they may think their triumphs and successes have been neglected by a process designed to highlight flaws and vulnerabilities. Sometimes a little well-deserved recognition can offset a whole lot of valid criticism in an audit report.

For internal auditors, it is absolutely necessary not only to be able to articulate a problem—what the potential impact is and how it can be fixed—but also to inspire corrective action. If we fail to inspire change, the entire audit process is a waste of time. And when it comes to inspiring change, there are times when a little recognition can be more motivating than a mountain of criticism. Emotion and perception are not things we talk about very often, but they can have a significant effect on how an audit report is received.

LIFE LESSON #27

For internal auditors, it is absolutely necessary not only to be able to articulate a problem—what the potential impact is and how it can be fixed—but also to inspire corrective action. If we fail to inspire change, the entire audit process is a waste of time.

Ultimately, I think, internal audit is judged by its ability to improve the organization, and to accomplish that, we can't afford to be tone deaf when dealing with others in that organization.

People want and need to feel appreciated and like to be recognized for their accomplishments, not just in our reports but throughout the engagement.

Ten Things You Shouldn't Write in an Internal Audit Report

The time-saving strategies discussed earlier are some of the most effective ways to ensure engagement reports are issued quickly. But one of the easiest ways to speed up a review is simply to avoid writing things that will inevitably be edited out of your reports. This is my "Top Ten" list of things you should *not* include in an internal audit report. Avoiding (or, in a few cases, at least limiting your use of) these things isn't going to save you huge amounts of time later, but doing so will reduce the degree of client push back and the number of unnecessary rewrites. You might even develop a reputation for clear and effective writing.

1. *"Management should consider..."*—Internal audit reports should offer solid recommendations for taking specific actions. When our recommendation is merely to "consider" something, it puts even the most urgent call to action at a disadvantage. No internal auditor wants management to respond to a recommendation with a simple, "OK, we'll consider it."

2. *Weasel words*—It's tempting to hedge our statements with phrases such as "it seems that" or "our impression is" or "there appears to be." But if you hedge too often, there's a danger that those reading your report will conclude that you are not presenting well-supported facts. They need to know they can rely on your findings and recommendations, but weasel words can make them sound more like hunches. If your report contains weasel

words, don't be surprised when those reviewing it kick it back and ask you for more information.

3. *Intensifiers*—Because they add emphasis, words such as "clearly," "special," or "very" might seem to be the opposite of weasel words. But these intensifiers are so non-specific they can amount to another type of weaseling. Intensifiers raise questions such as, "'Significant,' compared to what?" and "'Clearly,' according to whose criteria?" If you use intensifiers too freely in a report, different readers of the same report may be left with very different impressions of what you're saying. Numbers such as 23 percent or $3 billion help tell a story, but just what does "very large" mean?

4. *Absolutes*—It's good to avoid vagueness, but there's a danger in words such as "everything," "nothing," "never," and "always." "You always" and "you never" can be fighting words to clients, prompting them to start looking for exceptions to the rule rather than examining the real issue. It's safe to say you tested ten transactions and none were approved, but it's overstating your results to state that transactions are never approved.

5. *Blame*—Internal audit reports are supposed to bring about positive change, not assign blame. We're more likely to achieve consensus when our reports come across as neutral rather than confrontational. The goal is to get to the root cause of the problem rather than call out the name of the guilty party. It's fine for a report to identify the party responsible for acting on an audit recommendation—not so fine to say, "It was Fred's fault."

6. *Failure*—Statements such as "Management failed to implement adequate controls" will invariably annoy those to whom we are looking for solutions. Simply

stating the problem, without assigning blame through words like "fail" or "failure," is much more likely to result in the needed corrective actions—while helping preserve our relationship with management for the next time we conduct an audit of their area.

7. *"Auditee"*—A few years back, people undergoing an audit were most often referred to as "auditees." But that's old school. Many experts now consider the term to have negative connotations and imply that the client is having something done *to* them by the auditor. Internal audit has become a collaborative process, and terms such as "audit client" and "audit customer" indicate that we are working with management, not working *on* them.

8. *Jargon*—Every profession needs a certain amount of specialized language, but the more we can keep technical jargon out of our internal audit reports, the clearer our message will be. If you use terms such as "transactional controls," "stratified sampling methodology," or "asynchronous transfer mode" more than once a page in your audit report, don't be surprised when you discover that some of those reading it check out before getting to the end.

9. *Subtle bragging*—While it is tempting in internal audit reports to use phrases such as "internal audit found" or "we uncovered," management will often bristle when you take credit for identifying something that wasn't all that well-hidden to start with. From their point of view, it's as if, after throwing them under the bus, you have it back up and run over them again.

10. *Verbiage*—You want those reading your audit to remember your recommendations and take action to carry them out, so don't bury them under mounds of pompous words

or bloated phrases. For example, don't say "by means of" when "by" will do, or "at the present time" when you mean "now," or "so as to" when "so" is the way to go.

I like to use the seventh-grader test when reviewing an audit report: if an intelligent middle-school student couldn't understand it, then it may be needlessly complicated. Take, for example, this 65-word sentence—from an actual internal audit report—that basically tells you, "Little things can add up":

> "During the aforementioned examination of the accounts undertaken by the internal auditors, the team evaluated the cumulative impact of individually immaterial items and in doing so relied on the assumption that it was appropriate to consider whether such impacts tended to offset one another or, conversely, to result in a combined cumulative effect in the same direction and hence to accumulate into a material amount."

Enough said; and then some.

Coping with the Review Process

Let's assume for a moment that you just wrote the world's first absolutely perfect draft of an internal audit report. It is clear, concise, accurate, fair, helpful, and everything else you could wish it to be. The tone is faultless, the issues are straightforward, and the recommendations are convincing. Not a comma is out of place.

Congratulations. You have just accomplished the impossible. But regardless of your report's perfection, it will now be edited.

Because internal auditors don't enjoy being criticized any more than our clients do, your first reaction to the editing of your report might not always be the best one. The key is to know how to cope with the editing process.

Extensive editing of your report can be frustrating, even disheartening, but it's important not to overreact. You need to understand why the edits were made and learn from those with more experience than you. If there is time in the schedule, you may want to put the report aside for a day or two so you can go back over the list of requested changes with a fresh eye.

If you still think the edits are inappropriate, the best approach is to make your case rationally and without emotion. Differences of opinion will always exist between internal auditors; there is merit in having more than one point of view brought to bear on an assignment. But if you can't come to complete agreement with the rest of the team about every word in the report, you may have to accept that the final decisions will be made by those ultimately accountable for the quality of the overall engagement.

The Fine Art of "Fence Repair"

When coaching internal auditors I remind them that audit reports are often the basis for evaluating management's performance, and unfavorable results have been known to cost executives bonuses, promotions, or even their jobs—especially if the report includes some sort of rating system. It may not seem fair, but as a result, adverse internal audits can damage relationships between internal auditors and management, a situation I call a "broken fence."

It is practically impossible to avoid breaking a fence now and then in our line of work. Internal audit reports must be accurate, and if an issue is significant enough to be in the report, it should not be negotiated out of the report or downplayed into virtual nonexistence. No matter how congenial you might be as an internal auditor, if you are doing your job correctly, there will be times when you have to "call it like it is," and that can create hard feelings or damage relationships. But no internal auditor can function effectively if surrounded by broken fences. A successful auditor learns, over time, the fine art of fence repair.

How do you mend broken fences? First, work tirelessly to avoid breaking them in the first place by anticipating the potential consequences of your internal audits and mitigating the damage before it occurs. For example, I have always discouraged the use of ratings in internal audit reports if used as a punitive measure, and I avoid inflammatory words and phrases. We should always strive to ensure that the tone of our reports doesn't lead to lingering animosity on management's part.

If a fence is broken, you need to consider a fence-mending mission. Here are a few of the strategies I have used to mend damaged relationships:

- Engage in frank and open discussion with the offended party or parties. Ask them to share with you their candid feelings about the accuracy or fairness of the report and what they think internal audit could have done better. (*Warning: These sessions can become contentious, so check your ego at the door.*)

- Solicit feedback from all of your internal audit clients using a customer satisfaction survey or similar mechanism. The ability to vent without a face-to-face confrontation can be therapeutic for some of those who take offense at your reports—and you might just learn about a few fences that you hadn't known were broken.

- Demonstrate genuine empathy when engaging someone who feels wronged by your report. If an internal audit costs someone their bonus, I put myself in that person's shoes when talking about our relationship going forward.

- Own up to your mistakes, whether made by you or the team as a whole. View mistakes as opportunities to improve.

Why should we care about broken fences? Well, as internal auditors we have to "live where we eat," and once a fence is broken, managers in that part of the organization will not want you auditing them again. And every internal audit this is conducted in that area from then on will occur under a cloud of mistrust and contention. Effective fence mending takes time. While a well-established relationship can be destroyed in a second, rebuilding trust between internal audit and a client is a slow process. If management thinks that trust has been compromised, it will take time for them to recognize again that our work is balanced and fair. So be patient; almost any fence can be mended.

CHAPTER 12

Innovation Drives Greatness

During my tenure at the Postal Service, the USPS OIG's office received quite a few requests for information from members of Congress—often on very short notice. One such request involved a U.S. senator concerned about the integrity of a relatively new postal money order called *DineroSeguro™* (Spanish for "Sure Money™"), which offered USPS customers an affordable and convenient method of transferring money to another country. At the time, customers could send as much as $2,000 per transaction per day from more than 2,000 participating post offices nationwide. Personal identification was required of anyone transferring more than $1,000.

The senator was concerned that these money orders were being used to launder drug money in violation of the U.S. Bank Secrecy Act. The fear was that criminals might be breaking large amounts of drug money into smaller, transferable amounts to keep the dollar amount below the threshold that would normally trigger added scrutiny.

The senator wanted to know if these money orders were being used for such illegal purposes—*and he wanted an answer in one week*! Given the incredible number of transactions and the geographic dispersion of the many facilities issuing these money orders, I was convinced that producing any kind of comprehensive report in a week was virtually impossible. But telling the senator that we could not provide the assurance sought within the requested time period would only heighten suspicions about the program and embarrass the USPS and the OIG.

I knew that, at the very least, we needed to develop some sort of preliminary analysis of *DineroSeguro*™ transactions. So I gathered the internal audit staff and said, "OK, guys, you've got to help me here. The senator wants this in a week. Let's do the best we can. Gather the data and let's put a report together. We'll send whatever we can get."

Three days later, the auditors returned and told me they had looked at more than 200,000 transactions.

"No, no," I said. "... Not how many money orders there were—how many did you actually examine?"

Their response? "Oh, we looked at all 200,000."

I was floored. How did they manage to do that? I asked. Turns out they made use of a software program called ACL that enabled them to electronically review every one of those money-order transactions and analyze them based on specific criteria. In three days, they were able to look at all 200,000 transactions and put together a well-written report.

Today, the use of data-analytics software such as ACL, Caseware's Idea, or modules in audit management systems such as TeamMate might not seem as remarkable as it did in 1999, but such technology solutions were clearly innovative at the time. Without it I could have put the entire inspector general's staff of 400 people to work on the problem, and in a week we still wouldn't have been able to examine every transaction. Such is the power of innovation.

Innovation in Internal Auditing

A major source of value generated by internal audit departments is the promotion of positive change within an organization—yet paradoxically, as a profession we seem to struggle with innovation when it comes to doing our own jobs. Internal auditors perform their work today in much the same way they did when I set out on my personal audit trail forty years ago.

Stagnation is not healthy in any business, and almost all of the processes that we audit, regardless of the industry, have been transformed in recent decades. But even as internal auditors enthusiastically talk up the benefits of positive change for their clients, they typically go about their business as creatures of habit, focused more on controls than on innovation. Controls are important, but as a strategy it does not add the most value to a company.

Internal auditors currently operate in a global business environment of increasing competition, technological advances, and downsizing. As a result, demand for internal audit's services is growing much more quickly than internal audit's capacity. Given these conditions, the profession's traditional practices may not be adequate; to stay relevant, internal audit needs to at least match the speed of the businesses it serves.

I don't mean to suggest that all internal audit departments resist change; the really great ones seem to thrive on innovation. But too many departments do resist change, while others still find it's all too easy to fall back on traditional techniques such as sampling, for example, even though new data-analysis tools can quickly analyze 100 percent of the transactions under study.

Fortunately, innovation doesn't always come about by accident; more often than not, it's the result of strategic thinking and hard work, so we can all benefit by analyzing the strategies that the great internal audit departments have developed to infuse the audit process with innovative thinking.

Because the demands on internal audit are growing faster than its resources, I am convinced one of the best opportunities for improvement is adding to internal audit's capacity and ability to deliver value without busting the budget. I like to think of strategies in these areas as *capacity multipliers* that can elevate the level of value we deliver and enable us to exceed our stakeholders' expectations.

Leading internal audit departments have been leveraging capacity multipliers in three main areas: strategic staffing solutions, transformed processes, and technology applications. Let's take a closer look at each of these.

Strategic Staffing Solutions

When I became FORSCOM's Chief of Internal Review in 1988, the department's staff had been pared considerably. Only four internal auditors remained in Atlanta to serve the headquarters of one of the largest military commands in the world. I knew that with appropriate resources, I could deliver value and prove to the command's chief of staff and controller that an investment in internal auditing would pay dividends. Yet I couldn't expect them to take my word for it; I would need to prove our worth if lost positions were to be restored.

So I set out to "beg, borrow, and steal" resources wherever I could find them. I persuaded the controller to loan me a qualified member of his staff and the HR department to give us a trainee position. I applied for and received an additional "individual mobilization augmentee"—an active duty U.S. Army reservist who is training on a part-time basis to prepare for mobilization. And I persuaded the command's chief of staff to authorize a "temporary over-hire" for one year. In just six months I had managed to double the department's staff; as a result, the number and quality of our audit reports improved and we were addressing more significant risks to the command. The changes were noticed by our stakeholders, and eventually we received permanent increases in the size of our staff.

With the constraints I inherited as a first-time CAE, I knew I had to think outside the box. The military's HR processes are notoriously slow, so I had negotiated the temporary staffing arrangements myself and simply taken the paperwork to HR for processing. I took an innovative approach to improving the capacity and capability of our department, and the results exceeded my most optimistic expectations.

Strategic staffing solutions often start by identifying capacity and capability gaps within the internal audit department. When a capability gap exists, functional and subject matter experts (SMEs) can provide additional insight for the whole internal audit department in highly complex or specialized subject areas, allowing engagement teams to "leap the learning curve." But few internal audit departments are large enough to have SMEs for every topic, so when the internal audit department doesn't have the necessary expertise, other, more affordable alternatives must be considered.

Leading internal audit departments address such staffing needs by leveraging SMEs from other business units within the company. In some cases, internal audit might simply consult the SMEs from other departments, though in many situations it may the expertise for a while, as I did at FORSCOM, ease short-term staffing constraints, undertake unique audit projects, or streamline engagements in remote locations. It's important to remember that this approach requires appropriate supervision and assurance that the temporary help is qualified and objective. For example, to ensure objectivity, I never allowed the FOSCOM staff member loaned to me by the command's controller to audit anything in the controller's area of operation.

Many companies have a "guest auditor" program, typically for the duration of a single engagement or a series of shorter ones. Guest auditors can provide functional expertise and institutional knowledge while serving as "goodwill ambassadors" for internal audit, returning to their regular jobs with a deeper understanding of internal audit's processes, risks, and controls. One large, global bank actually requires professional employees in certain areas of the operation to serve as guest auditors in internal audit before they can be considered for a promotion.

If you like the idea of a guest auditor program, remember that turnabout is fair play. Internal auditors can gain valuable operational experience through staff-rotation programs that enable them to work temporarily in other divisions. These kinds of programs place extra demands on internal audit's management, but in the long run, they enhance people's knowledge of risks and controls throughout the organization.

When gaps in staffing can be filled by less-experienced help, you might consider internships. Vigilant supervision is required when working with interns, but ongoing supervision and quality control should be integral to every internal audit program, and internships serve a dual purpose by also fostering talent for the future.

When the budget allows, third-party internal audit providers are a flexible form of augmenting staff. Third-party services are commonly used to acquire foreign-language or other specialized skills, expand geographic coverage, provide a quick response to fast-changing conditions, or otherwise add flexibility to a department's operations. I used third-party providers to augment operations while I was with the Army, USPS, and TVA.

In most cases, if your audit committee sees a need for third-party resources to address significant risks, money will be made available. But even with limited budgets, internal audit departments can take advantage of resources outside the company. For example, some audit departments "borrow" internal auditors with specialized skills from other organizations such as companies in their geographic area or industry. Confidentiality issues can be a challenge, especially if industry-specific skills are needed. But imagine what could be gained if, for example, an internal audit department with advanced information-security expertise needed an internal auditor with strong derivatives experience—while a neighboring internal audit department with strong derivatives experience needed help with an information-security engagement. Borrowed internal auditors can be especially helpful after a natural disaster or other major emergency. And while such exchange programs seem to occur more often among large companies, there's no reason smaller companies can't benefit by swapping internal auditors with hard-to-find skills.

Keep in mind that, if an internal audit department wants to take advantage of one or more innovative staffing solutions, its success depends on three things:

- Ensuring participants' qualifications and credentials
- Ensuring their objectivity as internal auditors
- Deploying the resources during the most critical phases of the audit—typically planning and reporting

TRANSFORMED PROCESSES

As mentioned previously, too many internal audit processes are not cost-effective. Many internal audit departments are dealing with excessive cycle times, outdated results, and a resulting diminished value that leads to stakeholder dissatisfaction. This gives us plenty of room for improvement. Here are the internal audit processes that I consider the best candidates for reengineering:

1. *Risk assessment*—Key features of a streamlined risk-assessment process include an efficient, documented methodology and integration of stakeholders' views and expectations. As noted in chapter 7, the most effective risk-assessment methods are continuous in nature rather than annual or semiannual events, and continuous-monitoring metrics can streamline the process considerably. Collaborating with other elements within the enterprise that also conduct risk assessments can also prove valuable. Management quickly develops "interview fatigue" if a stream of professionals show up to ask them over and over, "What keeps you awake at night?"

2. *Audit planning*—As discussed in chapter 9, key features of an efficient and effective engagement-planning process include:

- Ensuring that risk assessment is the primary basis for determining objectives, scope, and specific tests
- Using a sound and consistent methodology
- Leveraging expertise from SMEs
- Incorporating advice from management and operating personnel
- Designing the engagement for efficiency, keeping the budget in mind

3. *Documentation and review*—These processes should follow a sound and documented methodology. It's important to keep in mind that internal audit, like any other process, can lose efficiency if it's over-controlled; more is not always better. As discussed in chapter 10, leading internal audit departments do not mandate incorporation of all documentation into the work papers, and they make use of digital-age technology in their documentation and review processes.

4. *Reporting*—As discussed in chapter 11, innovative internal audit groups are experimenting with a variety of ways to enhance the timeliness of their reporting.

5. *Monitoring and follow-up*—Follow-up is too often neglected. If internal auditors report significant risks to the audit committee but do not ensure that management addresses the risks appropriately, then they are actually raising the audit committee's risks rather than lowering them. Consider, for example, those companies that had compliance problems with the U.S. Foreign Corrupt Practices Act; the consequences were invariably more severe if senior management and the audit committee knew about the problem but took no action. We must design efficient, timely follow-up systems that conform

to professional standards and that leverage management assertions on the status of corrective actions in decisions about the timing and methodology for follow-up.

DEPLOYING TECHNOLOGY

We live in a time of revolutionary advances in technology, and internal audit systems are included. Innovative new tools continue to emerge, enhancing internal audit's ability to provide value to today's stakeholders.

Internal auditors must learn to leverage this new technology as a capacity multiplier. Such technology comes with a price tag, and in tight budget situations, internal audit departments will have to learn to do more with less. But the digital technology and electronics now available and in development will, over time, help auditors spend less time planning, documenting, and reporting—and more time auditing.

One innovation underway for more than a decade now is the linking of data analytics to audit automation systems. This allows internal audit departments to continuously monitor the various controls for potential fraud detection so important to risk management and risk assessment. As Brian Loughman, a partner and fraud expert at Ernst & Young LLP, points out:

> The audit industry also needs to use technology proactively and to its full potential in order to mitigate fraud risks. At the current time, it is being used as a reactive means for fraud investigations. Technology tools can enable awareness into the effectiveness of an organization's anti-bribery and anti-corruption compliance programs. New technologies will allow internal audit to increase effectiveness in mitigating risks of fraud and to bridge the gap between policy and practice.[1]

Another important innovation will be integrating audit technology systems into today's smartphones and computer tablets. Younger professionals, in particular, expect to be able to use such devices to tie together the audit community and facilitate the sharing of ideas. These innovative technologies will soon be put to work in nearly every career field, and audit executives may need to showcase technology during the recruiting process if they want to attract the brightest young professionals in the job market.

Training in technology-based audit tools must also become a part of the education process at our universities. Some schools are already incorporating technology into their internal audit curricula. DePaul University, for example, includes technology training in both its master's and undergraduate programs for accountants and internal auditors. And the newly released third edition of The IIA's textbook, *Internal Auditing: Assurance and Advisory Services*, includes a case study about technology in every chapter.[2]

Principles of Innovation

Innovation is such a broad and subjective topic that distilling ideas about it into a single chapter is difficult. I have already offered some tactical suggestions focused specifically on internal auditing. But what about fundamental principles of innovation? I personally like what Google's chief social evangelist, Gopi Kallayil, calls the "nine core principles of innovation":

> **Innovation comes from anywhere**—The source of creative knowledge is not the purview of senior executives. It can also come from the bottom up.
>
> **Focus on the user**—If you obsess about results, you are missing the real point. Focus on your customers and stakeholders, and the results will materialize.
>
> **Aim to be 10 times better**—In other words, think big or go home! Don't strive for marginal improvement. Seek transformational change.

Bet on technical insights—Using the technical insights of your department or enterprise will serve you well.

Ship and iterate—Striving for perfection will leave you at a competitive disadvantage. The last 80 percent of time is often spent striving for 20 percent improvement.

Give employees 20 percent time—Employees should be given 20 percent of their work time to pursue projects about which they are passionate, even if it is outside the core job or core mission of the department or enterprise.

Default to open processes—Be transparent about your processes. Leverage the collective energy of all of your clients and stakeholders to obtain great ideas.

Fail well—Do not attach a stigma to failure. If someone is not failing often, he or she is probably not trying hard enough.

Have a mission that matters—We should each believe the work we do has an important impact on the people and enterprise that house them.[3]

Necessity Can Be the "Mother of Innovation"

One of my favorite examples of innovative thinking by internal auditors came from the audit team we stationed in the Middle East at the conclusion of the Gulf War and Operation Desert Storm. Military operations had ended, and all of the equipment we had leased—very rapidly—after Iraq's invasion of Kuwait had to be brought back to the United States so it could be returned to the contractors from whom it had been leased. Deadlines were rapidly approaching if we wanted to avoid extending these expensive leases for another year.

The equipment had been secured in supply containers hooked to big-rig trucks for ground transport. But now that the equipment was no longer being used, the containers were laid out on thousands of acres near the port from which they would be sent home. The Army internal auditors there were asked to help identify the equipment—based only on the serial numbers marked on each container. This had to be done quickly so the containers could be loaded on ships to begin their voyage back to the United States.

If the auditors had taken their clipboards and started walking down the aisles between the large containers, it would have taken them days or weeks to complete the task. But one of the auditors noticed that the top of each container was clearly marked with a large serial number, and so the team came up with the idea of taking a series of photographs of the sprawling equipment-staging area from a helicopter. Once the team had the photographs, they pieced them together to create a virtual aerial shot of the entire staging area. The team could then pinpoint the exact location of each container that held equipment with soon-to-expire leases. Thanks to the internal auditors' map, logistics officers were able to swiftly locate and load the high-priority containers in a fraction of the time it might otherwise have taken.

Incredibly innovative! That's the kind of out-of-the-box thinking we need more of, and the truly innovative internal audit departments are already showing us ways we can put this type of thinking to work within the internal audit profession.

Innovation Is About Behavior

We have all seen examples of businesses that set up systems and processes designed to achieve certain things, only to fail because the corporate culture did not allow them to succeed. This can happen anywhere in an organization, including within internal audit. In one department, new tools such as automated work papers might be celebrated, while in another they might be viewed with dread. The culture within an internal audit department can make the difference between success and failure in transforming its audit policies and practices.

When focusing on culture, two dimensions are important: the leadership and the team.

THE LEADERSHIP

"Tone from the top" is fundamental to the success of innovative programs. To ensure that a business realizes value from its investments in innovations, its leadership must foster a culture that will facilitate change. However, as PwC's internal audit thought leaders have observed, the behaviors that underpin that type of culture are very different from the traditional management paradigms.

THE TEAM

Highly innovative employees are known for certain behaviors, including curiosity, courage, creativity, appropriate risk taking, lateral thinking, collaboration, and open-mindedness. The challenge for management is to ensure that performance evaluation and reward systems encourage these behaviors and that the corporate strategy and organizational values both explicitly and implicitly reinforce the importance of these behaviors.[4]

FROM	→	TO
Command and control	→	Empowerment and trust
Information is power	→	Openness
Delegation	→	Participation
Single-answer solution	→	Multiple answers and experimentation
Fear of failure	→	Learning from failure
Risk aversion	→	Sensible risk taking
Rigid work practices	→	Flexibility and adaptability
Individualistic	→	Team-oriented
Perfection	→	Trial and learning

Challenges to Implementing Innovations

A study undertaken in the 1990s, *Enhancing Internal Auditing Through Innovative Practices*,[5] had two objectives: to collect and describe a sample of innovations, and then synthesize the information to identify characteristics and issues common to the implementation of such innovations. The study's ultimate purpose was to help readers set in motion some innovation of their own internal audit departments.

Case-study participants reported encountering similar problems when implementing change. But they also detailed strategies that had solved the problems. While it has been a few years since the study was conducted, I think some of the observations have enduring value:

Staff resistance to, and readiness for, change

Even where there was agreement that change was needed, every internal audit activity in the study faced some degree of resistance from staff to the selected innovations. Staff expressed concern that workloads would increase, that unrealistic expectations would be imposed, that they were being asked to perform tasks usually not associated with internal auditing, or that the innovations would dilute the core mission and purposes of internal auditing. In some cases, staff said it was unprepared to assume new roles, especially when those roles involved higher levels of responsibility and accountability.

The internal audit organizations in the study used certain strategies to address these concerns, including:

Attrition

Open communication

Staff involvement

Investment in training

Meaningful roles in creating change

Modified hiring practices; hiring of more senior staff

Introduction of mentoring programs

Not only did the internal audit departments have to build staff support for the changes, they faced challenges obtaining support for their innovations from the organization's business units and corporate leadership. In every case, internal auditors adopted a marketing perspective, working to inform their customers about internal auditing and to demonstrate the value they added to the corporation. Another effective strategy was gaining the endorsement of outside consultants or experts. A longer-term but powerful means of building corporate support was to increase crossover between internal audit and business-unit employees.

General lessons learned about the successful implementation of innovation within internal audit departments included:

1. Innovations always have costs.

2. Reception to innovation within the internal audit organization will be mixed.

3. Reactions outside the audit organization will be mixed as well.

4. Audit clients should be carefully chosen for the selected innovations.

5. Innovations need ongoing support.[6]

Innovators Unafraid of Risk

Innovative organizations don't just enable out-of-the-box thinking; they embrace it. At one large American technology company, for example, an award is given annually for the "Failure of the Year." The employee who launched the boldest project, even if it failed, is highly praised. It's certainly an unusual award, but it does send a clear message—that the organization rewards taking well-planned, strategic risks even if they don't pan out.

During my brief hiatus from internal audit in the 1980s, I served on a cost analysis team that prepared extensive studies about the cost of moving Army bases and closing Army installations. The Army had just begun to downsize at the time.

On one of my first projects, I created a cost model designed to show how much it was going to cost to move family housing quarters from point to point, such as moving from New York to Anchorage, Alaska. This was quite early in my career, and personal computers were still relatively new. I was really proud of my model—and that my numbers were being put into major cost studies.

But one day I suddenly discovered that I had made a mathematical error. My years of training as an internal auditor had taught me that everything had to be very precise, so I went to my boss and said, "I made a mistake. My model is wrong; the numbers it is cranking out are wrong."

"How much is it off?" he asked.

"A hundred-thousand dollars," I replied.

At which point he responded, "It's not a decision-altering error; don't worry about it." He was right. We were looking at cost options totaling in the hundreds of millions of dollars. While my error seemed like a lot to me, it would have no effect on the overall decision.

His reply was a liberating moment for me. I realized that, as internal auditors, we can get so hung up on the details that we forget to think about what it is we're really trying to achieve. As innovators, if our ultimate goal is to develop strategies that hit home runs for our stakeholders, we have to be prepared to strike out occasionally.

LIFE LESSON #28

As internal auditors, we cannot be so paralyzed by fear of failure that we are unwilling or unable to innovate.

CHAPTER 13

Small Stones Can Cause
the Biggest Waves

Early in my internal audit career, I learned how easy it is for something relatively insignificant to have far-reaching ripple effects. In this chapter, I will share examples of how findings in an audit report can be taken out of context or assigned much greater significance than warranted. And I will share what I learned about ways to manage such situations.

In chapter 2, I mentioned working on an internal audit team in Southern California in the early 1980s. We examined the processes used to reactivate Fort Irwin, an old, sprawling Army installation in the desert. Fort Irwin had not been fully active for many years, so a lot of infrastructure had to be built and materials acquired before soldiers and other employees could begin working there.

As part of the audit, the team reviewed the contracting procedures used for acquisitions and the administration of those contracts. In summarizing some of our observations, I noted that purchasing officials had bought an extraordinary number of trash cans—so many, in fact, that the trash cans would outnumber the civilians and soldiers stationed there. The cost of those trash cans was certainly not "material" when compared with the overall expense of activating the installation, but I chose it as an example in my report to illustrate the need for stronger controls when planning such purchases.

Despite the relative insignificance of the error, senior officials reviewing the audit report were quite upset and reacted vehemently to my observation. I was surprised at first, then realized that, even though there wasn't a substantial amount of money at stake, the example was a vivid indication of a lapse in the project's internal controls. Our report actually identified several other, larger instances of waste and inefficiency, but the senior officials seized on this relatively obscure incident—with potentially severe consequences: I remember the head of contracting sitting across a desk from me, tears in his eyes, telling me that he had been informed he would likely be fired because of the trash cans.

In my view, management had overreacted. What I didn't realize at the time, that early in my career, is that it was symptomatic of a type of problem of which all internal auditors should be aware: sometimes the most ordinary obscure audit findings will generate the most extraordinary reactions.

The "Small-Stone Effect"

Every internal audit professional looks forward to career milestones—those "big impact audits" that we can look back on later with the satisfaction of knowing our work made a real difference. Whether it's in internal auditing or life in general, we all aspire to make this world a better place, even if only in small ways. What makes internal auditing especially rewarding is that it can bring about significant change in an organization, the kind that prompts senior management and board members to sit up and take notice.

But often it's the little things, not the big ones, that attract the most attention. We assume that those who will read our reports will assess the significance of our findings and recommendations using the same criteria as we do, but that's not always the case.

Occasionally, the facts we communicate in our reports draw attention or spark the imagination in ways we did not anticipate—and all heck breaks loose, as it did at Fort Irwin. I call this phenomenon the "small-stone effect," when something with the financial significance of a rounding error starts out as a ripple, like those made by a pebble tossed in the water, but grows into a tsunami of overreaction or negative publicity as it spreads outward.

I soon began to connect the dots when much-bigger examples of the small-stone effect starting bursting on the public scene just a few months after my Fort Irwin experience. A series of embarrassing incidents began to spring from U.S. Department of Defense reports on overspending. These cases, involving seemingly insignificant purchases beginning in the early 1980s, received a huge amount of media attention and generated a public backlash against what was viewed as wasteful or inefficient spending by the military:

1. THE PENTAGON'S $435 HAMMER

In 1982, the U.S. Navy issued a sole-source contract to an electronics company that included a line item for a $435 claw hammer.[1]

There were underlying cost-allocation and accounting reasons for the hammer to carry a price tag of $435. But to the average taxpayer, able to buy a hammer for less than $3 at the local hardware store, the figure seemed outrageous.

2. THE NAVY'S $660 ASHTRAYS AND $400 WRENCHES

In May 1985, the Navy began investigating bills of $660 each for two aircraft ashtrays purchased in February 1983 and bills of $400 each for two socket wrenches bought in June 1984.

The Navy directed its "price-fighters" team to do a "should-cost study" of the purchases to determine the real value of the items.[2] But the news media and public had a field day with the story.

3. The Pentagon's $640 toilet seats

In the mid-1980s, information provided by whistleblowers and reported by an oversight group, the Project on Military Procurement, exposed the seemingly exorbitant purchase of $640 toilet seats for use in the Navy's P-3C Orion antisubmarine aircraft.[3]

Once again, word of the expense set off huge waves—including a presidential news conference to address the uproar.

While I was certainly not involved in these high-profile "small-stone" examples, I was soon to have more first-hand experience with this phenomenon.

The Gold-Plated Telephone Poles

The year I returned to FORSCOM after attending the Army War College was a relatively uneventful one. We built an outstanding internal audit team at FORSCOM headquarters and, as the CAE, I focused on directing the team's work for our stakeholders.

But the following year, in the spring of 1993, the FORSCOM chief of staff asked me to look into whether officials in another Army organization had appropriately used FORSCOM funds to equip an engineer unit stationed at one of their installations for Operation Desert Storm two years earlier.

During my visit to that host installation, I noticed some new telephone poles laying in a nearby staging area where supplies for the engineer unit were stored. A quick review revealed that the poles had been purchased with FORSCOM funds, but had never been shipped to the Middle East and were now available to improve the host installation's infrastructure. This smacked of "gold plating," a term often used to describe the actions of anyone who takes advantage of an emergency or contingency to buy supplies or materials for routine use at a later time.

I reported my observations to the FORSCOM chief of staff and shared them with FORSCOM's chief engineer. What I didn't expect was that a member of the FORSCOM engineer staff would share my report with officials of the other organization's host installation. Although the telephone poles were a relatively inexpensive item, my small ripple generated a giant wave of controversy between the two organizations. At one point, the host installation's commander, a two-star general, said I was unprofessional, irresponsible, and didn't know "the first thing about war fighting." In the end, everyone calmed down, but it was another example of a small stone causing giant ripples—in this case because someone inferred that we had questioned their integrity or motives.

The Grand Canyon Stamp Error

In 1998, I moved to the big leagues of government auditing when I joined the U.S. Postal Service Office of Inspector General (OIG). It didn't take long for me to experience firsthand the small-stone effect on the national stage. I was driving to work one morning in May 1999, when I was assistant inspector general for audit, when I heard a radio report about the Postal Service's new stamp honoring the Grand Canyon. But it wasn't about the stamp's debut—it was about how the stamp misidentified the location of one of the county's most-recognized landmarks, the Grand Canyon. The U.S. stamp's caption: "The Grand Canyon in Colorado." Unfortunately, the portion of the Grand Canyon pictured on the stamp was in Arizona.

The error generated lots of media attention, including stories in *USA Today*, *The Washington Post*, and scores of other newspapers. While we did not disclose the error, the USPS inspector general and I knew we needed to move swiftly to identify the cause of the mistake and recommend ways to avoid similar errors in the future. Fortunately, all of the incorrect stamps were still physically inside the printing facility. Management acknowledged that, because of human error, existing control processes had not been followed and subsequent revisions to the original artwork had not been formally approved before the start of production. Management reiterated its commitment to follow existing control processes in the future.[4]

Again, this error did not waste a material sum of money, but the attention it drew damaged the Postal Service's reputation. As the USPS' auditors, we were also "under the gun" to identify the cause of all the big waves.

Alien Presence at TVA

When I was inspector general at the Tennessee Valley Authority (TVA), we received a complaint that some employees were using their computers for a study-at-home initiative called the Search for Extraterrestrial Intelligence, or SETI. Software had been downloaded onto the employees' computers, allowing them to help sort through radio-signal data collected by the giant Arecibo radio telescope in Puerto Rico.

When TVA's employees signed up for the program, they received a free computer screensaver—and software that allowed the study-at-home coordinators, when the employees' computers were inactive, to access TVA computers via the Internet to help search the radio signals from outer space that could indicate the presence of extraterrestrial intelligence. No proof of intelligent life elsewhere had been found to that point, and we recommended that the software be removed.

It was a fairly modest report. We identified nineteen employees who had been using their work computers for the SETI project. We shared the report with management and, as required by law, I included a reference to it in my semiannual report to Congress. The local newspaper picked up on it and, lo and behold, it went viral. I remember it making the news in Australia.

At the time, the SETI computer program, which came from the University of California at Berkeley, had been downloaded by more than three million computer users worldwide. The TVA security breach was a violation of the agency's written policy but was not considered a serious one. We recommended that administrative action be taken against the employees—something IGs, though not internal auditors, occasionally do. TVA employees were warned that any future computer security violations could result in dismissal. No evidence of damage to TVA's computer network was found, and TVA managers conducted a computer security awareness campaign throughout the agency.[5] But another small stone had a ripple effect around the world.

The "Lavish" Satellite Office

Although my tenure at TVA was shorter than my other stops along the audit trail, it was packed with action in terms of small stones triggering tsunamis in the form of media coverage. While reaction to the SETI software had been global, the most intense media coverage from a TVA audit conducted during my time there involved "lavish" spending to refurbish a satellite office for the agency's board of directors.

TVA's headquarters is in Knoxville, Tennessee, but many of its operations are based about 100 miles west of there, in Chattanooga. In 1999, it was decided to relocate and upgrade a small office in Nashville, about 180 miles from Knoxville. The new space would include an office for the agency's chairman and a boardroom. At the request of a member of Congress, we initiated an audit of the project and identified several examples of furnishings that generated intense publicity and strong congressional reaction—including a $53,000 conference table, a $42,000 glass backdrop, and $326,000 spent to transform hickory trees from President Andrew Jackson's historic home in Nashville into paneling for a new library adjacent to the chairman's office.

Once again, for an agency the size of TVA, with an annual budget totaling $8 billion, these were not material examples of waste, and no fraud was detected. But that audit report created waves of publicity.[6]

The Nashville office was front-page news in Knoxville and Chattanooga, and the region's largest newspaper, the *Atlanta Journal-*

Constitution, did an in-depth report. Members of Congress weighed in too, calling the project a "boondoggle." The public was incensed that a government-run utility that helped set their electric-power rates was spending money on such extravagances. There was little I could do about this as the IG; I had an obligation to report the findings. We avoided characterizing the expenses, though others had no problem attaching terms such as "excessive" and "dubious."

It's a Matter of Perspective

I wish public officials and the media had paid as much attention to some of the truly consequential examples of waste and ineffi-ciency in the internal audit reports I worked on or supervised during my years in government auditing. But if you analyze enough audit reports about $640 toilet seats and $53,000 conference tables, you can begin to see why certain findings resonate with stakeholders and the public in ways that much more important findings do not.

People's reaction to findings of waste or inefficiency in an inter-nal audit report have less to do with the amount of money involved or the consequences of the error than they do with how much they identify with the problems, usually in a negative way.

So, what's an internal auditor to do? I learned early on the impor-tance of putting my report observations in perspective. If the amount of money involved is not material and the problem or error cited is not systemic and poses no threat, then the observation may not even warrant inclusion in the report; you can still review such issues with management so they can be addressed without the turbulence of the "small-stone effect."

LIFE LESSON #29

Put audit findings in perspective so those reading them can weigh the comparative importance or consequence of each error or problem.

If disclosure is appropriate, then the finding should be discussed in a way that clearly places the issue in perspective, especially if you anticipate media coverage or other public scrutiny. If you observed nineteen cases of employees using their computers inappropriately, as we did at TVA, you should probably mention that it was out of a total workforce of almost 13,000 people. If you find two instances of a wasteful activity within an organization, you should indicate the total number of instances examined, or express the wasteful activity as a percentage of the whole. The SETI security breach at TVA was a minor issue—barely a paragraph in a thirty-five-page report sent to Congress. But the idea of TVA employees using government computers to search for space aliens was manna for the media. The topic became a source of fierce debate on the Internet, and I even received a few pieces of hate mail.

Ironically, little was said in the media at the time that the same semiannual report to Congress also identified more than $70 million in questionable or unsupported costs or funds that could have been put to better use. It was the pebble, not the rock, that made the big splash.

A final note: just because the internal audit finding that triggers an outsize reaction is a "small stone" that didn't merit all the attention doesn't mean it didn't merit corrective action. For example, a couple of years after the audit of its refurbished Nashville office, TVA announced that it was relinquishing the space—for a savings of more than $1 million a year.[7]

CHAPTER 14

No One Is Immune
to Ethical Lapses

When I was FORSCOM Chief of Internal Review, an internal review director in one of our subordinate organizations called one day seeking my advice. Her department had identified several problems during an internal audit of the organization's IT function. The IT director had concurred with the report and asked if the lead internal auditor for the engagement could help the IT office implement the audit recommendations. The internal review director asked if I thought temporarily assigning the internal auditor to the IT department to help with the corrective actions would pose a problem.

"I don't think you want to do that," I responded. "It will impair your department from going back to audit in this area later on. But you and your organization need to make that call."

I soon forgot about the conversation—until a few months later, when I received a subpoena from a federal judge to appear before a labor relations hearing. An employees union had filed a grievance against management for allowing an internal auditor to undertake work that the organization's IT staff could have performed. I was called to testify regarding any breach of Government Auditing Standards (Yellow Book) resulting from the action.

I was puzzled because I had assumed the internal review director had decided against allowing the temporary transfer. When I asked her why she had ignored my advice and agreed to let the internal auditor work in IT, she dropped an even bigger bombshell. She said IT made her a promise: "We'll give you all new computers if you send this auditor over to help us out."

"I couldn't pass that up, right?" she added.

I was almost speechless at the news. "You do realize that now your decision impairs you even more?" I responded. "How are you possibly going to go back and audit the IT department when you are on the hook because they gave you all those computers?" The internal audit director hadn't done anything illegal, but her twin decisions—to allow an internal auditor to help implement recommendations in a department her office would have to audit again, and to accept equipment from that very department in exchange for the favor—were serious ethical lapses that had tainted her office's reputation.

LIFE LESSON #30

It is internal auditors' ethical duty to avoid even the appearance of a conflict of interest.

When Ethical Lapses Turn Serious

"Ethics is so boring, until you go to jail," was how a recent post on Twitter summed up the problem some people have with ethical standards. I am not suggesting that internal auditors are likely to end up in jail, though it is not unprecedented, unfortunately. What we do need to worry about is how often our behavior and our decisions fail to promote an ethical culture within our profession and the organizations we serve.

The first decade of the twenty-first century had no shortage of high-profile ethical lapses in the corporate world. Remember Enron Corporation? It is still the poster child for corporate fraud and ethical lapses in this country, and its collapse was partly responsible for passage of the U.S. Sarbanes-Oxley Act of 2002. WorldCom was another massive accounting fraud at about the same time; IIA members who worked there played a key role in exposing the fraud in 2002. Similar ethical meltdowns were reported at Parmalat, Adelphia, Tyco, and elsewhere.

The reality is that corporate executives often get caught in ethics scandals, but to our shame the internal auditors responsible for monitoring these executives and the operations they manage have ethical lapses too. In recent years, CAEs in several instances have been caught up in foreign-bribery scandals or covering up frauds.

My heart stands still each time such a case appears among the headlines on the Internet, because I fear the damage it can do to our profession. "How is a company supposed to avoid corrupt payments when the individual tasked with finding out about corrupt payments [the internal auditor] and reporting them to the Board of Directors is himself complicit in the bribery scheme?" Howard Sklar asked in a recent blog post on Forbes.com.[1]

People often ask me what keeps me awake at night as the head of The IIA. It isn't our operations or our finances, and it isn't concern about our professional standards or certifications coming under attack. What keeps me awake at night is the possibility of more headlines about internal auditors violating our Code of Ethics.

Ethical misconduct is not a matter of isolated instances. During a roundtable of about seventy CAEs at one of our annual IIA General Audit Management Conferences, I asked those present, "Have you ever discovered or witnessed ethical lapses within your own internal audit function?" Nearly one-third of the CAEs acknowledged they had.

What Causes Ethical Lapses?

Various motivations have been mentioned for the ethical violations that internal auditors in recent years have been accused of committing, including these:

- Loyalties to other senior executives

- Desire to protect the organization

- Protection of career opportunities

- Conflicts of interest

- Lack of courage and integrity

- Disregard of The IIA's Code of Ethics

Sometimes, internal audit professionals do things that raise questions about their ethical behavior without them even recognizing the situation as an ethical lapse. If we are professionals and expect others to think of us as such, then we must hold ourselves to an ethical code. And it has to be about more than just *how we do our work;* it has to be about *how we behave.*

If you are a certified internal auditor (CIA), then you are already aware of The IIA's Code of Ethics. A vast majority of internal audit departments have compliance with the code somewhere in their internal audit charters, which require them to comply with the code and other mandatory guidance in The IIA's International Professional Practices Framework (IPPF). But I wonder how often we as individuals really think about the code or what it means to our work.

LIFE LESSON #31

Recognize the risk that unethical behavior poses to the internal audit profession, and work hard to prevent the kinds of activities that discredit us individually and the profession at large.

The stated purpose of The IIA's Code of Ethics is "[t]o promote an ethical culture in the profession of internal auditing." It has two components: the Principles and the Rules of Conduct. The Principles express the four ideals to which internal audit professionals should aspire as they go about their work, while the Rules of Conduct describe twelve behavioral norms.

Let's take a quick look at the four principles:

1. *Integrity*: The integrity of internal auditors establishes trust and thus provides the basis for reliance on their judgment.

2. *Objectivity*: Internal auditors exhibit the highest level of professional objectivity in gathering, evaluating, and communicating information about the activity or process being examined. Internal auditors make a balanced assessment of all the relevant circumstances and are not unduly influenced by their own interests or by others in forming judgments.

3. *Confidentiality*: Internal auditors respect the value and ownership of information they receive and do not disclose information without appropriate authority unless there is a legal or professional obligation to do so.

4. *Competency*: Internal auditors apply the knowledge, skills, and experience needed in the performance of internal audit services.[2]

BLIND SPOTS

At first glance, complying with the four principles may seem like a straightforward proposition. But many ethical lapses are committed as the result of "blind spots."

I became familiar with this concept only recently when I picked up the book *Blind Spots* by Max Bazerman and Ann Tenbrunsel.[3]

Most of us would think that people who commit fraud or some other ethical breach intend to do so. But Bazerman and Tenbrunsel suggest that, when people have a vested interest in seeing a problem in a certain way, they are no longer capable of objectivity. And that, I think, presents us a serious challenge as we try to keep our personal ethics compass pointing in the right direction.

My good friend, Cynthia Cooper, who wrote the Foreword to this book, writes extensively in her own book about the challenges she experienced while working at WorldCom.[4] At one point near the end of the book, Cynthia warns her readers:

> Guard against being lulled into thinking you're not capable of making bad decisions. Each of us is imperfect and must protect against giving in to temptation. Keep in mind that what is legal and what is ethical are sometimes different.[5]

Real-World Blind Spots

I have faced ethical dilemmas during my career, and I have seen blind spots at work within the internal audit profession. As you read through the following real-life scenarios, ask yourself, "Have I ever seen or done that?" That's the trouble with blind spots.

I. "THEY REALLY AREN'T GOOD POLICIES ANYWAY."

An auditor was assigned to review his organization's travel policies. He soon discovered that his client was not conforming to policies requiring purchasing the lowest airfare and documenting receipts—but he also knew the internal audit department was not complying with the policies either. He had to decide whether to include the violations in his report or ignore the problem.

As he struggled to make a decision, he rationalized, "They really aren't good travel policies anyway." That rationalization led him to reason that internal audit wasn't following the policies because they weren't sound business practices. So he didn't include the issue in the final report.

I stumbled on this omission as we were conducting a quality assurance assessment of that very same department, so I called the auditor in to talk about the situation. "You know, I couldn't write them up because we don't follow the policies either," he said.

That auditor's attempt at an explanation is the kind of rationalizing that can start early in your career if you decide, "There is some room for interpretation as we go through an internal audit if the results might somehow reflect badly on us."

2. "CONDUCTING THE AUDIT DURING THE HOLIDAYS WILL DISRUPT THE BUSINESS."

I was once involved with a company whose business cycle was particularly heavy around the annual winter holidays, from mid-December into the early part of January. It was in an industry that had to deal each year with an inherently high degree of risk involving its logistics and customer service during the busy holiday period.

The team working on an internal audit of the company in this particular instance was aware of operational problems. There had been problems in prior years regarding deadlines and merchandise shipments during the busy year-end season. Internal audit had rated the risk as high in the company's annual risk assessment, and so the audit plan specified that the engagement team would complete the current audit during the holiday season, because that's when the problems usually occurred.

But when it was almost time for the audit to start, several internal auditors asked the department director, "Are you really going to make us work on Christmas Eve and Christmas Day, and those days right around the holidays? On those days, we want to be with our families."

At the same time, the director was hearing from the company's operating managers, "For goodness' sake, don't audit us that week, because that is the most difficult week of the year from an operations standpoint. Your auditors will disrupt things if they come then."`

The audit director was finally persuaded to delay the audit because his staff also had plans for the holidays, and he had originally planned to vacation during the holiday season too.

The director issued a memo to the operating officials, stating, "We will defer this audit due to potential disruption of your business operations."

Whether the decision to delay was the right one or not, the audit director hadn't come clean; he was at least as influenced by his team's desire for time off as he was by the effect that a holiday audit might have had on the business.

If the internal auditor in this case felt strongly that the audit should be delayed, he should have stated that he was deferring it for both reasons—at the request of the operating managers being audited *and to allow his staff to spend the holidays with family.* Sure, he came across as the good guy to management and his auditors, but I believe his approach raised serious ethical questions because it wasn't completely honest.

3. "I DON'T RECALL IF THIS WAS GOING ON WHEN I WAS HERE."

A woman who joined the internal audit department after working in one of the company's business units was scheduled to audit the area where she had previously worked. Internal audit policy was that you cannot be involved in an audit of your former work area for at least a year, but the proper amount of time had passed.

During the audit, she found several control deficiencies that she suspected had existed when she was responsible for that area. She also knew that if she reported the deficiencies, the current audit client would likely say, "But this was going on when you were here."

She feared damage to her reputation if she put herself in the position of defending her earlier work; at the same time, she didn't want to ignore the problem completely in her report because it was clearly documented in the work papers.

So she reasoned to herself, "I don't know whether or not this was going on when I worked there, but that's irrelevant—I don't think it's important enough to include it in the report as a finding. We will just put it in the back of the report in a section that we call *other areas for management consideration.*" She did not bury the deficiencies, but she didn't treat them as she would have had she not had a prior connection to the problem before joining internal audit.

In the preceding scenarios, the internal auditors did not view their actions as unethical—they rationalized their decisions and convinced themselves and others that they were in the best interest of the department or the organization.

4. "It's not worth damaging a personal relationship."

An internal auditor assigned to lead the audit of a business unit managed by a close friend—the best man at his wedding—unearthed problems during the audit. Significant risks weren't managed well and controls weren't effectively implemented. The auditor knew that if he reported the problems, they could damage the friend's reputation or destroy a long friendship—or both.

So he told himself, "I can't exactly bury the issue or ignore it. But if our objective in doing the audit is to improve the organization, why do we have to write a big finding about it, embarrass the guy, and make him look bad in front of everybody else in the organization? I'll just talk to him about these areas. I'll walk him through these deficiencies and he will fix them. He will understand that this is something that should be taken care of and, because we found it during the audit, it *will* be taken care of."

In the internal auditor's mind, he had addressed the issue properly. The problems were fixed, after all. But he might have viewed his reasoning in an entirely different light if it had been another auditor doing this. All internal auditors have friends and established relationships throughout their organization. We discussed the value of these relationships extensively in chapter 5, but it's important to remember that personal relationships can easily create conflicts of interest and lead to ethical lapses.

5. "FIRST IMPRESSIONS ARE LASTING IMPRESSIONS."

A new CAE who was not yet fully aware of the skills and capabilities of the internal auditors in his department decided that, based on an updated risk assessment, a team needed to audit the deployment of a new system in the IT department.

So the CAE turned to one of the department's young internal auditors, who had already been in to meet him (only some of the staff had yet briefed him on what each of them was doing), and said, "I need you to lead this audit, and here is what we need to do."

The young auditor knew full well he wasn't the best choice to lead an IT audit; there were others in the department who had done such audits before and were much more qualified to lead the engagement. But he wanted to make a good impression, so he said, "Yes, sir."

I saw the audit report later, during an external quality assessment, and I didn't find anything that I thought was particularly deficient in it. But I also knew that, because I had reviewed information about the internal audit department's staff and their qualifications, this internal auditor wasn't even in the top five on staff who should have been assigned the audit.

The IIA's Code of Ethics precludes internal auditors from taking on work for which they are not qualified. Had this auditor behaved unethically for not having said, "I'm not the best person to do this"? In his case, he wanted to prove that he *could* do it, and he wanted to lead the team. But was his decision ethical?

6. "BETTER NO EXTERNAL QUALITY ASSESSMENT THAN A BAD ONE."

IIA Standard 1312 states:

External assessments must be conducted at least once every five years by a qualified, independent assessor or assessment team from outside the organization. The chief audit executive must discuss with the board:

- The form and frequency of external assessment; and

- The qualifications and independence of the external assessor or assessment team, including any potential conflict of interest.[6]

That standard has been in place now for more than twelve years, yet many internal audit departments have never undergone such a review—*even in cases where the requirement is clearly spelled out in their charter and approved by the audit committee.*

In a case I observed a few years ago, a CAE who had been in place for some years had every intention of getting the external quality assurance (EQA) assessment done. She knew it needed to be done and was preparing for it, but just a few months before the EQA was to be scheduled, a new CFO and a new audit committee chairman joined the company.

The CAE faced a dilemma. "I don't know how the EQA will come out," she thought to herself. "We haven't had one before and I don't want to risk having the results make internal audit look bad in front of a new audit chair and CFO. That would undermine the credibility we hope to build with those key stakeholders." So she decided to delay the EQA for a year; in her mind, it was better to have no EQA than to have an unfavorable one.

7. "OF COURSE WE CAN ABSORB THOSE REDUCTIONS."

The economy was slumping and the CAE was informed that internal audit's budget was to be cut by 25 percent, which would require eliminating 25 percent of the department's staff positions. The CAE knew that would mean delaying or cancelling several internal audits of high risk areas scheduled for the coming year, but the CEO and the

CFO were clear about the situation, saying, "This is it; don't argue. Take your share of cuts just like everybody else in the organization."

When the audit committee was made aware of the internal audit staff cuts at its next meeting, the chairman turned to the CAE in executive session and said, "Now, let's go back to these reductions that we talked about earlier. Will the reductions impair your ability to address the key risks that we have told you are important to us?"

The CAE knew the answer was more than a simple *yes* or *no*. There were risks that fell into that category that he would not be able to cover adequately, but he would have real problems with the CFO and the CEO if he told the audit committee his team may not be able to address all of its important concerns. So his response to the chairman's question? "No, no. As I said earlier, we can take these cuts and still get the job done," he said. "We'll be fine."

This is a situation many CAEs will face eventually. During a recent CAE forum, I asked those present how comfortable they would be in sharing information with the audit committee that they had not discussed first with the CFO or their direct supervisor.

I was surprised at the responses. Quite a few willingly said, "Yeah, I would not be comfortable doing that at all."

But that's what they pay us to do. That's why CAEs get the "big bucks," right? To make tough calls and to acknowledge, "I know this isn't going to go down with the CFO or the CEO. But I'm going to be asked a direct question by the audit committee chair, and I cannot hide this or lie."

8. "I WON'T FIT IN LATER IF I DO THAT NOW."

A lot of audit departments have positioned themselves as a pipeline of talent to their companies in recent years by employing developmental or rotational programs at the end of which internal auditors rotate into a business unit. I think there is real value in sharing internal audit's talent with other departments and becoming a source of such talent within the organization. But some departments have set up very rigid rotational cycles, so that the individual knows that he or she will come into the internal audit department, spend approximately three years there, and then be expected to move into another business unit.

Some companies that have a rotational audit staffing cycle want the internal audit staff to have the chance to audit the areas within which they next want to be assigned. I see an inherent conflict of interest if auditors are assigned to an engagement in a business unit into which they hope to be rotated; it challenges their objectivity. I was talking to some of the staff attending an internal audit conference a few years ago, many of whom were earmarked for transfers soon to new positions within their companies. I asked them, "Have you audited the area you want to go into?"

"Yes," one of them replied.

"What did you do?" I asked. "Did you find any problems in that area?"

"Yes. I identified some internal control design and implementation issues," he said.

So I asked, "Did you report them like you normally would?"

His response: "I was concerned, because if I put them in the report, I was worried that maybe the folks in the department would decide I might not be a good fit. But we worked that out. I talked them through it and they fixed the problems, so I didn't need to put them in the report."

A disturbing theme runs through this and several of the other scenarios. When a conflict of interest exists, whether we recognize it or not, we aren't likely to handle audit issues the same way we would if we were truly objective about the situation. The first step to avoiding such ethical lapses is to know a conflict of interest when we see it.

9. "Don't Worry, Be Happy."

The Foreign Corrupt Practices Act (FCPA) prohibits the bribery of foreign officials and employees who work for foreign governments. But while bribery is illegal, the federal law allows for *facilitation payments,* which are payments "designed to facilitate the execution of clerical or ministerial government tasks" such as making provisions for telephone, water, and power service; police protection; mail delivery; business permits; and inspections tied to contract performance or the shipment of goods.[7] Thus, the line between bribery and facilitation payments can sometimes be very thin.

In a case I didn't experience personally but which made national headlines, a company's internal audit staff had documented numerous FCPA violations. The CAE conferred with the company's general counsel, who read the draft report and probably responded with something like, "You can't say that."

The CAE's likely response? "Well, this is what we found."

So they met again about a week later. "Our legal staff has looked at everything you gave us," the general counsel said, "and I want to assure you that you don't have any FCPA violations. What you found were merely facilitation payments, which are perfectly acceptable. If you put these matters into the audit report, you are going to look bad. You will force us to go in front of the audit committee and tell them that you don't know what you are talking about. You need to take our advice here and back off."

So the CAE did just that, though he came to regret it. The general council spun it in a way that made the CAE back away, essentially reassuring him that legal and management was OK with the payment while simultaneously threatening to confront him before the audit committee in a battle of wills management expected to win. But that didn't change the facts as the CAE's staff knew them to be. When the bribes were eventually exposed and a scandal ensued, the company ended up in much more trouble than if everyone had addressed the issue openly—back when it was first identified by internal audit.

This particular type of blind spot is certainly not limited to FCPA compliance. Have you ever been in a conversation with general counsel, or another corporate executive with specific expertise in audit results, during which you were pressured to take a different view of something or word a report differently? I'm not blaming general counsels; they get paid to do one thing, we get paid to do another. But we shouldn't defer to them if we are sure of our findings and recommendations.

After those run-ins with the general counsel, I would hope that I pressed forward and presented both points of view to senior management and the audit committee. Looking back later, I would not want to be the one who had said, "They are the lawyers; I'm just the auditor."

IO. "THIS COULD WIPE OUT THE WHOLE COMPANY."

Occasionally, an internal auditor comes upon significant financial reporting fraud. For example, earnings have been manipulated or overstated. In some cases, the external auditors didn't catch the issue, so internal audit needs to blow the whistle on the problem.

If you are new to this profession, I recommend reading *Extraordinary Circumstances* by Cynthia Cooper. In 2002, Cooper and her team of auditors uncovered a $3.8 billion fraud at WorldCom, the then-giant telecom company. It was, at the time, the largest accounting fraud in U.S. history. WorldCom's CFO and others in the company clearly pressured Cooper to not report the enormous ethical violations she had discovered.[8] They gave her all kinds of excuses, such as—it's just a temporary thing; they insisted it's going to reconcile. So determined was she to not get caught in the ethical quicksand that she had her staff work at night to keep them out of top management's sight. Cooper knew what the discovery would do to the company, her colleagues, and the community, but she also understood her ethical obligations.

MODELING ETHICAL BEHAVIOR

I like to think internal auditors really are guardians of trust for the organizations they serve. Yes, individual auditors have ethical lapses, but as a profession, we strive to behave ethically every day. It's what I call the vision of internal audit leadership in ethical organizations.

Having been fortunate to meet many internal auditors who exemplify ethical leadership, I have identified seven traits that ethical internal auditors share:

Seven Traits of Ethical Internal Auditors

First and foremost, ethical internal auditors are *honest*. They don't lie, they don't conceal; they are open and transparent. They would correctly be described as *honest individuals*.

Second, they are *courageous*. They are willing to make really tough calls. As an internal auditor, if you never have bad news to deliver, something is seriously wrong, because no matter how well-run your organization, mistakes always occur and there's always room for improvement. You must have the courage to say what needs to be said.

Third, they are *accountable*. If they do something wrong or bad, or have a department that isn't meeting standards, they admit it and take responsibility for the problem.

Fourth, they are *empathetic*. They realize they are auditing *other human beings* as well as business units and departmental processes. Those people face challenges and are wrestling with issues of their own, and ethical auditors work to understand and share their experiences and feelings—without sacrificing their objectivity toward the job at hand.

Fifth, they are *trustworthy*. They are dependable, good, and effective as well as honest.

Six, they are *respected*. They are seen by colleagues throughout the organization as someone to be admired for all of the other ethical attributes they bring to their role.

Finally, they are *proactive*. They do not wait until after an ethical transgression has occurred to speak up if they see it happening.

Throw a Flag Before the Play

In American football, which I enjoy watching, the referee sometimes throws a penalty flag even before the ball is snapped and the play begins. For instance, the referee will throw a flag for a "false start" if certain players on offense move before they're supposed to.

Throwing the flag before a play starts because something isn't right is, I think, exactly what internal auditors should do in their role as corporate watchdog and fiduciary and a key part of their organization's conscience.

More than once in my career, I have needed to interrupt the process to warn of an impending mistake or a crisis in the making in the hope it would spur management to action and prevent the problem. I think I added far more value to the organization by doing so than if I had simply shown up afterward and written a report critical of the situation and recommended what could be done differently next time. For me, it was the ethical thing to do.

I have been discussing with others in recent years the various roles internal auditors can play across what I called the "ethics continuum." On rare occasions, when internal auditors get directly involved in a fraud or unethical conduct, they become *accomplices*; on some occasions, they are partly at fault simply because they sat on the sidelines and failed to expose the inefficiency, waste, fraud, or mismanagement. I consider such internal auditors to be *spectators*.

Most of the time, however, internal auditors are *referees*. They monitor the series of plays that constitute the normal course of a business' operations and blow a whistle or throw a flag only when they identify a mistake or transgression that has already occurred. They objectively determine whether a penalty, foul, or other infraction has occurred.

Just as a football referee will interrupt the game if there are too many offensive players in the huddle, and a baseball umpire won't allow a pitcher to throw until a hitter is settled in the batter's box, internal auditors must be willing to call for a halt to the action if they see a problem looming. I call this being part of the *conscience* of the organization.

A good example of when internal auditors should have blown the whistle or even thrown a penalty flag was the rolling out of the federal Affordable Care Act's health-insurance website—healthcare.gov—in the latter part of 2013. The site's debut was a fiasco, with consumers unable to research or purchase medical coverage for days, weeks, or even months. The software and related systems obviously had not been ready for prime time, which suggests that opportunities may have been missed for someone to sound a warning. Either auditors in the U.S. Department of Health and Human Services' Inspector General's Office weren't proactive enough in warning agency officials of potential risks or failures, or they were less than effective in preventing the disaster once they had warned the agency.

The time for internal auditors to get involved with complex IT systems for business or government is when they are being designed; if the auditors observe lax planning, internal controls, or system design, the time for them to speak up is before the new equipment is deployed. Waiting until deployment risks the reputation of the very organization they are entrusted to serve. It is internal audit's obligation to raise any concerns early on and often, and to proactively warn management of the potential of failure.

In the case of healthcare.gov, the result was a big, long-running public relations nightmare for a presidential administration that had placed much emphasis on health-care reform.

CHAPTER 15

Always Remember—
We Are Auditing People Too

Today's internal audit professionals must understand the possibilities and flaws of human nature so they can develop strategies to maximize the possibilities and minimize the pitfalls in their day-to-day work.

As a young internal auditor, I concentrated on learning the technical skills needed to succeed in the profession. I learned early in my career about the importance of developing a comprehensive plan at the beginning of every engagement, documenting the work, and writing a clear, concise report. I also learned about the business area I was auditing and how it operated. These skills served me well throughout my career, but I can honestly say that learning the technical skills was easy compared with cultivating the people skills that I also needed to succeed.

Over the course of my career, I have led or served on scores of audit teams involving an array of industries and military or government operations. In doing so, I noticed that, regardless of the type of function or operation I was auditing, they had a lot in common in the way the people behaved. Overall, the many people whose operations I have audited have been good, decent, and hard-working professionals. Many had thankless jobs at which they toiled tirelessly without complaining. But I also learned that human nature is a complex thing. You can't always take what people say or do at face value.

Smart People Can Do Dumb Things

It's easy for internal auditors to become intimidated when auditing an area led or filled with intelligent, seasoned professionals. They can dazzle you with their deep understanding of the area's operations, and their knowledge can appear unassailable. Yet I have frequently observed some of these bright folks doing some pretty dumb things. For example, I have uncovered instances when violations of internal controls in their area turned out to be deliberate circumventions that they had instigated in the belief that their experience or expertise didn't warrant such controls. Don't assume smart people always do smart things.

How do internal auditors accomplish their work in the face of such uncertainty about their clients? New auditors tend to see the world in black-and-white terms: "Should we do an audit?" "Should we issue a finding?" "Am I maintaining a healthy degree of professional skepticism?" For many new internal auditors, such questions point unerringly to a single, yes-or-no answer. But with experience, an internal auditor comes to realize that the answers to these kinds of questions are more nuanced than that. The issue is not merely whether we should perform an audit, but whether risks in the program, function, or activity warrant an audit compared with other areas where the risk may be greater; whether sufficient resources are available; and how soon the audit would be needed. The issue is not just whether to report a finding, but how significant the finding is relative to others in the audit, and how strongly to word the description if we write one.

The same thing applies when we attempt to draw the line that separates a healthy amount of professional skepticism from harboring unwarranted suspicions about the people we audit and the areas they operate. Professional skepticism means we take nothing for granted—we continuously assess audit evidence and other information, and we question what we see and hear. We take pride in never missing a clue or warning sign, in remaining alert for hidden messages that other auditors might miss. It is a quality that is essential to our work as auditors.

The flip side of skepticism is that too much can actually hamper an internal audit's effectiveness. I once had a hyper-suspicious auditor who worked for me; he always assumed his clients were guilty of something and his primary job was to "blow the whistle" on them. Not surprisingly, his working relationships with management and with me deteriorated over time; managers were less than forthcoming during risk assessments and audit engagements when he was involved. His overly suspicious nature eventually led to a breakdown in communication and weaker audits.

The written performance goals for many internal auditors might include initiatives to building working relationships with key stakeholders and fostering business partnerships with management. Unfortunately, the need for professional skepticism means we can never completely trust the very people in our organization who want us to be their partners. And that means management is less likely to think of internal auditors as trusted advisers, especially when compared with their "partners" in other departments.

Finding an appropriate level of professional skepticism and knowing how to express it are critical to an internal auditor's long-term success. One size does not fit all: some internal auditors rely more on building relationships, while others are more inclined to "dig out the truth" in the form of hard facts. The trick is to exhibit *just the right degree* of professional skepticism in any given situation.

If only we had a standardized rating system for determining our level of skepticism! Unfortunately, accurate and flexible ratings are not likely to appear anytime soon. Imagine a checklist with statements such as, "The client seemed nervous and was sweating profusely. Add three skepticism points." Or, "The sample size was statistically significant. Deduct one skepticism point."

For me, the secret is simply to approach each situation with an open mind and communicate in a way that demonstrates my underlying trust and confidence in management. I will still need to ask tough questions, but I will also use tact in asking those questions—and in deciding when and how to ask them.

"Trust but verify" was a signature phrase of U.S. President Ronald Reagan, who used it often in the 1980s when discussing superpower relations with the former Soviet Union. For internal auditors, "trust but verify" should be words to live by. We need to demonstrate trust in our co-workers—and to continually verify that our trust is well-placed.

Good People Can Do Bad Things

When we think of fraud, we tend to associate it with nefarious characters who deliberately set out to do something they know is wrong. But as discussed in chapter 14, many of the fraudulent or illegal acts uncovered by internal auditors are committed by otherwise decent people whose blind spots caused them to lose their way. Often these people were under extraordinary financial or personal pressures outside the workplace; they often rationalized their initial actions and didn't intend for them to morph into a full-blown fraud. As internal auditors, we should not assume that everyone is doing bad things, but our professional skepticism should remind us that even good people can do bad things.

The first time I stumbled onto a fraud was during my very first internal audit job at Trust Company of Georgia in Atlanta. Working in the bank's internal audit department proved to be a great experience for me. I learned about internal audit processes and the financial services industry. I had a chance to participate in branch office audits, which were fascinating. These were surprise audits; the internal auditors assembled about two blocks away from the designated branch office, and right at closing time the team showed up to look for any concealments, fraud, or violations of company policy. The audit also included the counting of all cash in the vault and on the premises.

Internal auditors were assigned to audit the tellers. Each teller had a "bank," so to speak, in their cash drawer. At that time, they had maybe $2,000 each in their banks to use throughout the day.

On one occasion, I began my teller audit with a female teller who did not even try to conceal what she had done with some of the money in her bank. "I have an IOU in here for some money that I've been using," she said. It was my first eye-opening encounter with fraud. I eventually learned that she was a sweet, good-hearted person who did not comprehend that she had committed fraud because, in her mind, she was going to pay the money back. She didn't think she was violating the law, but her actions could have resulted in a charge of embezzlement.

WHY DOES FRAUD HAPPEN?

Interviews with people who commit fraud reveal that most of them don't set out to commit such a crime. Often, they take advantage of an unexpected opportunity; many times, the first fraudulent act was triggered by an accident—perhaps they mistakenly processed the same invoice twice, didn't correct the problem, and discovered that no one noticed. After that, their fraudulent acts were deliberate and became more frequent. Fraud investigators talk about the 10-80-10 law, which states that 10 percent of all people will never commit fraud, 80 percent will commit fraud under the right circumstances, while the remaining 10 percent actively seek opportunities for fraud. So internal auditors need to stop the 10 percent who are out to get us—and strive to protect the 80 percent from making mistakes that could ruin their lives.[1]

The Association of Certified Fraud Examiners' (ACFE's) 2012 Report to the Nations on Occupational Fraud and Abuse estimated the cost of internal fraud worldwide totals $3.5 trillion in U.S. dollars, or 5 percent of all enterprise revenue.[2] And, as we all know, internal fraud is only part of the picture.

Everything is moving faster these days, including fraud. A rogue employee with a smartphone and a sufficiently weak control environment at work could transfer significant sums of money offshore in the blink of an eye. According to the ACFE, the average fraudster takes $140,000 out of a company before the crime is detected.[3] Little of that money is ever recovered.

LIFE LESSON #32

Never forget that every audit client you encounter is a person faced with varying sets of circumstances in their lives with the potential to react either positively or negatively to those circumstances.

To be good at detecting fraud, internal auditors must understand exactly what it is. The IIA's *Standards* defines fraud as, "Any illegal act characterized by deceit, concealment, or violation of trust. These acts are not dependent upon the threat of violence of physical force. Frauds are perpetrated by parties and organizations to obtain money, property, or services; to avoid payment or loss of services; or to secure personal or business advantage."[4]

Detection technology is advancing as rapidly as fraud, with real-time transaction monitors exposing anomalous patterns that might otherwise have gone undetected. Systems for collecting tips—for example, fraud hotlines—and a robust internal audit function have also proven effective at detecting fraud. But detection should never be the first line of defense.

In fraud, as in medicine, an ounce of prevention is worth a pound of cure. Donald R. Cressey, the late criminologist, is credited with identifying the three ingredients necessary for fraud—motive, opportunity, and rationalization—that are known collectively as the fraud triangle.[5] With appropriate risk assessment and controls, an organization can effectively shrink the "opportunity" side of the triangle. But if you don't know what you're looking for, how will you know when you've found it?[6]

IIA Standard 1210.A2 specifies internal audit's responsibility in the fight against fraud:

> "Internal auditors must have sufficient knowledge to evaluate the risk of fraud and the manner in which it is managed by the organization, but are not expected to have the expertise of a person whose primary responsibility is detecting and investigating fraud."[7]

As a federal inspector general, I had a key responsibility to prevent and detect fraud in my agency. I was fortunate to lead a well-resourced cadre of auditors and criminal investigators, and, looking back, I give us high marks for our ability to detect and investigate fraud where it had already occurred. But I continue to think that the real opportunities lie in fraud prevention. Leveraging our knowledge of the risks and getting in early—before the fraud can occur—would add so much more value for our stakeholders.

People Appreciate Recognition for Accomplishments

As internal auditors, we are told from the outset that our job is to provide assurance on the effectiveness of risk management, internal controls, and governance. But too often we forget to balance our assurance by reporting the good as well as the bad. Instead, our final reports head straight for the findings on inadequate risk management, internal controls, and so on. Many internal audit reports are submitted with no genuine recognition of management's accomplishments during the audit period, which serves to reinforce our reputation of being "professional fault finders." Based on my experience as an internal auditor, I have concluded that people are looking for an objective assessment of their operating areas. They understand we have a job to do, but they believe such an assessment includes some recognition of the things they accomplished or did well. Including a "management accomplishments" section at the beginning of an audit report can pave the way for general acceptance of our findings and the recommendations for corrective actions that follow.

THE IMPORTANCE OF RECOGNITION

Recognizing people's accomplishments both within the internal audit function and in management and executive positions within your organization goes a long way toward fostering an atmosphere of cooperation and support. Mutual recognition is an essential condition of effective relationships; to recognize someone is to acknowledge implicitly or explicitly that you are aware of and value their contribution to the enterprise.

Taking time at the onset of an internal audit engagement to show appreciation for your client can set a positive tone for the entire engagement. Inserting a management accomplishments section at the front of an audit report can generate a positive response to the report.

As the leader of an internal audit team, you should recognize the achievements of your team as a matter of course. Sincere and honest praise lets employees know you value their efforts. Such simple acts take little time but provide many benefits. With a few encouraging words and a pat on the back, you recognize and reinforce desired performance behaviors. And an employee who feels appreciated is likely to continue those desired behaviors.

As a CAE, you should make sure your staff knows they are valuable members of the organization. Praise creates and reinforces a positive self-image in employees, making each one feel like a winner.

This is particularly helpful in confusing or unclear situations, when an employee is trying to do the right thing but is uncertain where their performance falls on the departmental scale.

I have also learned that employees under stress also need a few words of praise to let them know they have done the right thing in a difficult situation. And when employees are assigned necessary but unchallenging tasks, they too should be praised for their contributions.

DON'T LET ASSETS BECOME LIABILITIES

Are you one of the best and brightest internal auditors in the profession? Are you dedicated, determined, and detail-oriented? Are you knowledgeable and self-reliant? Do you always seem to have the correct recommendations for complex audit findings? Great! But be warned: your professional assets can become liabilities.

These kinds of qualities will usually serve you well in the internal audit profession. But all humans are fallible and, as we discussed earlier, our "blind spots" are often closely linked to our strengths. I have identified several traits usually possessed by successful internal auditors that, under certain circumstances, can become liabilities:

Are you the most dedicated auditor in your department?

Maybe you work long hours to verify just a few more facts or to interview just a few more people. Normally, that's a plus for a career. But if your passion for completeness gets out of hand, you soon may find that "scope creep" gets the better of you and undermines the timeliness of your engagements (as discussed in chapter 9). There are only so many hours in a day, so try to keep in mind that spending too much time on one internal audit might not leave enough time for the next one.

Are you widely admired for your industry experience and technical knowledge?

If so, you bring important strengths to the department and your career. But nobody's knowledge is complete, and the more experienced you are, the more likely you may begin to rely on outdated information should the situation change. Auditors viewed as "experts" are also tempted to live up to their reputations by offering opinions even when they don't have all the facts. And even the world's most experienced experts need help on occasion—though it may not occur to them to ask. A second opinion doesn't make you any less of an expert, and the people you ask for help will probably be flattered that you sought their opinion.

Is your work highly accurate?

It's great to have a reputation for professional infallibility. But everyone makes mistakes sometimes, and the danger is that, if you are almost always right, it may be difficult for you to spot or admit your mistakes when you are wrong. After all, you haven't had much practice!

Are you extremely detail-oriented?

Attention to detail is important in internal auditing, but if you are particularly detail-oriented, you may become so tightly focused that you lose track of the bigger picture. Too much detail in an audit report can actually hamper the delivery of its most important messages. We usually only need to tell the reader what time it is—not how the clock works!

Are you passionately committed to bringing about positive change?

Enthusiasm is important. But if you are particularly determined to bring your audit clients around to your point of view, remember that they may also have valid points to make. Internal auditors should consider new evidence fairly, even when that evidence doesn't appear until the closing meeting—or later.

When the Finger Points at Us

Recent media coverage of corporations charged with violating U.S. anti-bribery laws has focused on the case of a globally recognized American company and the prosecutors who are scrutinizing a draft internal audit report to determine whether the company's executives ignored or tried to conceal the report's findings from the company's audit committee. If so, prosecutors think it could help show intent—a key element in obtaining criminal charges.

Cases such as this raise an important internal audit issue that I think the profession needs to talk about: if an internal audit report is ignored or suppressed, whose fault is it?

One of a CAE's most fundamental roles is to ensure that members of management and the company's audit committee get the information they need to make sound decisions. When someone prevents important internal audit findings from reaching the audit committee, it undermines key tenets of our profession.

I recognize that many forces are at work when audit information is suppressed. The decision to censor or suppress important information rarely starts with the CAE. Still, ultimately it is the responsibility and obligation of an organization's internal auditors to make sure essential information gets to the audit committee in timely fashion and in enough detail for management and the committee to take appropriate action. Sure, there are obstacles, and at times the challenges can be formidable—but rarely is the task impossible.

The IIA's *Standards* is clear: audit reports must include significant risk exposures and control issues, including fraud risks, governance issues, and other matters needed or requested by senior management and the board. Communication must be accurate, objective, clear, concise, constructive, complete, and timely. When the CAE thinks senior management has accepted a level of residual risk that may not be acceptable to the organization, she or he must discuss the matter with senior management; if the matter is not resolved, the CAE must report the matter to the board of directors for resolution.[8]

The *Standards* is clear. But to me, this issue is more than a matter of complying with professional standards; the CAE has a professional and moral obligation to ensure that the audit committee is advised if there is evidence that the organization may be a party to criminal wrongdoing.

Management and the audit committee bear some of the responsibility for ensuring free and open communication between the organization's auditors and the audit committee. Audit committees that rarely meet privately with the CAE ought to consider rethinking the meeting agenda. If reporting lines don't ensure internal audit's independence, objectivity, and organizational stature, it may be time to reassess internal audit's reporting relationships.

Failures Can Be Keys to Success

I have concluded over the course of my career that how people respond to critical internal audit reports often speaks volumes about their character and probably indicates how they deal with criticism or disappointment in other parts of their lives. I think you can tell a lot about a person's character by the way they respond to any setback. I can't tell you how many people I've known over the years who have suffered setbacks and never recovered; they just couldn't resume their forward progress and get on with their professional or even personal lives.

In my career, I can recall at least three times when I dearly wanted a promotion or an assignment and didn't get it. Each time, failure presented me with a choice: I could press on and thrive, keeping an eye out for further opportunities, or I could quit—literally or figuratively—and let failure define me.

For me, there was really no choice. I can tell you that, every time I failed to get something I wanted, I chose to persevere and wound up achieving much greater success down the road thanks to opportunities I might have missed had I been granted that earlier wish.

But don't take my word for it. History is full of similar examples.

Growing up, Milton Hershey thought he wanted to be a printer. I can't help but wonder what s'mores would be made with today if he hadn't been fired and then signed on as an apprentice candy maker.

Walt Disney's dream of becoming an ace reporter was shot down in flames when an editor at the *Kansas City Star* fired him for "lack of creativity."

Thomas Edison's teachers told his parents he was stupid.

And Steve Jobs' greatest successes at Apple came only after he had been forced out of the company he had founded and then brought back into the fold to run the technology giant.

I was devastated when I did not even make the list of finalists for the deputy controller's job at FORSCOM a few years after I had left the giant Army command to work at the Pentagon. I look back today in awe at how limiting such a "prestigious" career assignment would have been for me and my subsequent career. I was disappointed again in 2004 when I was not selected to be The IIA's next president. Yet I could not imagine the past decade without the exhilarating experience of having been a part of the internal audit practice at PwC!

As you consider your career in the internal audit profession, never be sure what is right for you and never give up—even when you think you have failed to achieve an important goal.

LIFE LESSON #33

Don't become paralyzed by fear of failure; a person's character and confidence are built mainly by overcoming adversity.

I'm not suggesting that failure guarantees future success. You should always examine the reason why you didn't succeed at something and seek to learn from it. Learning is one of the greatest gifts of failure. I'm just urging you to not let failure define you. I would say the same of success. Both are merely mile markers on your personal audit trail. Neither is a destination.

As Rudyard Kipling, author of *The Jungle Book* and *Gunga Din*, put it in his poem "If":

> If you can dream—and not make dreams your master;
> If you can think—and not make thoughts your aim;
> If you can meet with Triumph and Disaster
> And treat those two impostors just the same ...
> Yours is the Earth and everything that's in it,
> And—which is more—you'll be a Man, my son![9]

Life and the careers we shape within it are really journeys. Speaking with the hindsight of almost forty years in the workforce, at some point I've probably questioned every career move I've made, but I don't regret any of them today. Take adversity as it comes and never quit; you will always learn more in life's valleys than on its lofty peaks.

Internal Audit Needs a Seat at the Table

Whenever I travel, I meet CAEs who long for an opportunity to secure the trust of key players within their organizations. The exact words vary, but the question they put to me amounts to this: "How can internal auditors get a seat at the table?" CAEs frequently seek my advice on the best way to secure and retain this seemingly elusive seat. Although there is no magic formula, I often share my thoughts on this professional quest.

When I arrived at TVA in the summer of 2000 as the newly appointed inspector general, I was mindful of the rocky relationship my predecessor had with the board of directors in the years leading up to his retirement.

As I contemplated a strategic approach for improving the Office of the Inspector General's relationship with TVA's board and executive management, I was struck by the current relationship, which was very much an *us versus them* arrangement—at least from management's point of view. For example, I knew that the board and management met regularly to review the giant electric utility's business strategy and its execution. I also knew that, as the inspector general, I was not invited to these meetings. I genuinely believed that getting a "seat at the table" was essential to better understanding the business and how its strategies and decisions were formulated.

In early 2001, I approached TVA's chairman and said I wished to attend the meetings as a non-decision-making participant. Not unexpectedly, he was very apprehensive. No previous inspector general had attended management's meetings (though no previous IG had a background in auditing). He said he was concerned my presence would have a *chilling effect* on the candid discussion of business issues and exchange of ideas. He also worried that management would view my presence as an attempt to gather audit leads that the OIG would then use to *cherry pick* areas of weakness in TVA's operations for targeting in our annual audit plan. I assured him I would not take advantage of such opportunities.

In the end, we agreed that I would attend these meetings on a regular basis, but I would not attend every meeting. I recall the tension in the room the first time I showed up for a meeting. Several executives made no secret of their mistrust of the OIG, even if they didn't know me. I took the opportunity early on to address the "elephant in the room" when I delivered a brief presentation on the OIG's newly formulated strategic plan and informed the executives that our vision was to be successful in "illuminating today's challenges and tomorrow's solutions" for TVA. I also noted that one of our strategic objectives was to "enhance communications with stakeholders and deliver services that meet their needs."

TVA executives remained skeptical, but I followed up on my pledge to work more collaboratively by "walking the talk"—particularly during these important meetings. Over time, I came to earn the trust of several key officials. When I retired from TVA in early 2002, more than one of the board members and executives who had initially been skeptical of my intentions indicated they had been proven wrong. They thought my seat at the table had helped improve relationships between the OIG and TVA's management.

LIFE LESSON #34

The process of earning a seat at the table begins long before you can pull up your chair. It starts with you building a trusting relationship with the organization's board and management.

Why a Seat at the Table?

For internal audit departments to deliver optimum value, the CAE and the department's staff need a keen understanding of the organization. Such an understanding must include how the business strategy is formulated and how risks are assessed and managed. A "seat at the table" is simply a label for the CAE's attendance at and participation in meetings and discussions with senior management and the board.

In seeking a seat at the table, it's most important that you first examine why you want to be there. Too often, internal auditors treat a seat at the table merely as a sign of success, which is a mistake. You must be at the table for the right reasons, not because you hope that being with senior executives will make others view you as a senior executive. Securing a seat at the table is a means to an end—not an end in itself. Not preparing for it in advance may damage, rather than enhance, your chances of delivering added value to the organization.

It's also a mistake to view a seat at the table as a source of audit leads. If you leave your first management meeting with plans for an immediate audit of the operating unit discussed that day, you may not be invited to the next one. You need to add value, not prevent others from talking freely. And I mean add value—management will benefit from our being at the table only if we are prepared to share, not just listen.

Think of guests at a dinner party: we want our hosts to invite us back. In the case of board and management meetings, it helps if we bring something fresh, interesting, and important to the discussion. Focus on making operations better in the future, not on past mistakes, and provide insight instead of hindsight. I understood that I would be more welcome at executive meetings of TVA if I was willing to share insights as the authority's inspector general on matters related to risk and control.

The table is not a training ground. We must be able to discuss critical strategies and business risks facing our organizations, and we must understand the organizations' core business and be aware of both internal risks and external factors affecting our industry. If we don't bring our own perspectives, we won't add value, but we must be able to defend our views by ensuring we fully understand the discussion.

Most internal auditors are prepared to offer such valuable insights long before they are invited to the table, because the invitation is usually the result of the relationships they have built throughout the organization. It's not what we write in an audit report that gets us to the table—it's what we do and say with management every day. Senior executives will want us there if they respect us and see us as knowledgeable, trusted advisers. By the time most internal auditors reach the table, they no longer see management meetings primarily as sources of audit leads because they are already fully informed on the subjects likely to be discussed.

Adding value at the table requires a different perspective from the one we use as internal control advisers. Most internal auditors can discuss internal controls for a new strategic initiative, but when management discusses the feasibility of such an initiative, controls may be just one facet. To act as senior management, we must add value to other parts of the discussion as well.

An important part of IIA Global's strategic plan in recent years has been to support internal auditors worldwide in their quest to obtain a place at the table. While The IIA can advocate granting auditors a seat at the table, ultimately decisions about the scope of the auditors' role will be made by boards and executives in the organizations where internal audit resides. Each CAE, therefore, must demonstrate the insight and ability to participate in the senior management team. Knowing what we want to accomplish and preparing diligently to accomplish it greatly increase our chances of getting to the table.

Are You a "Trusted Adviser"?

Many CAEs and internal auditors also long to be "trusted advisers" within their organizations. They want management and the board to seek them out for advice on matters involving risk, control, and governance based on their understanding of the business and an assured level of trust that they have fostered over time.

But aside from possibly making us feel good about ourselves, what does it really mean to be a trusted adviser?

If becoming a trusted adviser were easy, we could simply prepare a sign or add a line to our business cards—surely management would then seek us out at the first signs of trouble, right? Not really. The term "trusted adviser" contains the two essential qualifications for achieving such status: we must be trusted and we must possess sufficient expertise to offer advice.

I often use a two-by-two matrix to illustrate the essential qualifications of a trusted adviser:

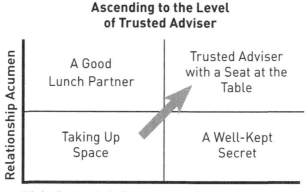

Ascending to the Level of Trusted Adviser

	Relationship Acumen	
A Good Lunch Partner		Trusted Adviser with a Seat at the Table
Taking Up Space		A Well-Kept Secret

Risk, Control, & Governance Expertise

As the graphic indicates, being a trusted adviser is a function of at least two broadly framed capabilities that CAEs must possess: risk, control, and governance expertise and strong relationship acumen.

First, CAEs must be able to leverage their expertise; they must have a keen understanding of the business and the industry's strategies and risks. They must also have a firm grasp of how effective internal controls mitigate risks and the board's and audit committee's roles in oversight. As discussed earlier in this chapter, without this kind of expertise, it is difficult for someone to provide meaningful insights, and a seat at the table will prove elusive.

A trusted adviser must also possess the relationship skills to build and sustain effective relationships throughout the organization. As we explored in chapter 5, relationship acumen is an essential attribute for successful internal auditors and CAEs. It is also an essential ingredient for building and sustaining trust. If you want to be a trusted adviser, there had better be a credible level of trust between you and your clients.

Possessing one of these attributes without the other will limit your potential as a CAE and typically leave you on the outside looking in when other executives are pulling their chairs up to the table. If you are competent but haven't built effective relationships, you will likely remain a well-kept secret—not seen as the go-to resource when management has concerns or questions. Your audit reports will likely be seen as clinical inventories of findings and recommendations, and management will probably not call you with requests to take on sensitive issues on their behalf.

On the other hand, if you and your team are seen as relationship experts but not very competent, you will likely be seen as little more than a great lunch partner. Management may find you and your team likeable but not much of a resource when they need answers to complex or difficult questions involving risk, control, and governance. The phone may ring—but only for rounds of golf.

Of course, the worst scenario is to be viewed as both incompetent and lacking in sold relationships with management. If that is the case, you are likely just taking up space and overseeing a weak compliance function. And you are not likely to remain in that role for very long.

Ultimately, the trusted adviser must be seen as having extraordinary expertise and someone with whom management has a strong and trusting relationship. These CAEs and internal audit staff are the ones that I invariably find in the high-performing internal audit functions around the world.

From Backroom to Boardroom

I would characterize internal audit's journey during the past decade as having taken it from "the backroom to the boardroom." Following those spectacular corporate failures in 2001–2002—and the subsequent regulatory and legislative response—internal auditing found itself front and center with the audit committee and other members of the board at companies around the world. The profession's rapid rise in stature is reflected in statistical studies. In 2002, for instance, The IIA found that only 55 percent of U.S. CAEs reported functionally to their audit committees, but by 2007, PwC found that the number had jumped to more than 80 percent. In recent years, internal audit's emphasis on assessing the effectiveness of financial controls has abated significantly. Given the shift in emphasis, I think there is a real threat that some audit committees may lose their newfound interest in internal auditing.

I suspect my view is one not shared by many. After all, it will be argued, corporate audit committees have much broader missions than mere oversight of financial performance and controls. But is that really true? From my experience during the past decade conducting quality assurance assessments of Fortune 500 companies, I was struck by how narrowly written audit committees' charters often were. In many instances, they were lifted directly from the sample audit committee charter promulgated by the New York Stock Exchange, which is heavily tilted toward oversight of the independent auditors as well as financial statement and disclosure matters. In fact, in the entire five pages of the sample audit committee charter, only two paragraphs are exclusively dedicated to oversight of the internal auditors. I have often found the emphasis in the audit committee charter was a reflection of the focus of its members, many of whom were primarily interested in receiving assurance from internal audit on the effectiveness of their company's financial controls.

Given the foregoing, I believe many CAEs face a significant challenge as they continue to rebalance their internal audit coverage to include greater emphasis on operational, compliance, and strategic and business risks. Their challenge will be to ensure the audit committee drives or embraces this direction and perceives the strong value that a comprehensive risk-based approach to internal audit coverage will bring. Otherwise, I fear some audit committees will grow bored with internal audit's coverage of nonfinancial risks.

As a profession, we have worked too long and hard to gain the stature we have enjoyed recently. Let's stay in the boardroom and retain the seat at the table with management, because it is there where we can share insight and foresight, which is valuable to those who lead the enterprise.

The Trail Ahead: From Hindsight to Insight to Foresight

When I look back on my journey along the audit trail, I realize how many of the lessons I learned on the way corresponded with change in our profession. The flexibility and resilience of internal auditors have been tested many times in recent decades. Some of the change has been evolutionary, but some has been revolutionary. Regardless, we are not what we used to be.

Not so many years ago, the "perfect" internal auditor was considered the one with twenty-twenty hindsight—the one who could go back in time through skillful use of records and interviews to uncover every mistake and report each misstep in exacting detail. Back then, we thought we best added value when we helped our organizations recognize past mistakes and avoid making them again in the future. At most companies, our primary role was finding out what had gone wrong. We were the hindsight experts.

Hindsight will always be important for internal auditors. We're often brought in to assess what happened, and when used well, hindsight helps others learn from experience and build expertise. But there are things hindsight cannot tell us. Hindsight alone could not have predicted the rapidly evolving legislation, the explosive technological growth, the mounting risks of cybersecurity breaches, the economic crises, or the many other changes we have experienced over the past few decades.

As the rate of change continues to accelerate, I can say with some certainty, based on the decades that I've been a part of this profession, that internal auditing has seen more changes in the past decade alone than at any other time in its history. And while clear hindsight continues to be important, one of the most fundamental ways in which we have changed recently is that we are no longer focused mainly on the past. In today's relentlessly evolving business environments, yesterday's ways of doing things are often not good enough. Our vision of the "perfect" internal auditor has been transformed: we have advanced from providing twenty-twenty hindsight to offering real insight into our organizations' risks, controls, and operations.

...To Insight

By moving from hindsight to insight, internal auditors exponentially added to the potential value of their services. As illustrated in chapter 4, insight has become a key element of internal audit's "value proposition." Hindsight analyzes the past to keep us from repeating our mistakes, but insight allows us to apply past lessons to new challenges. With insight, internal auditors are no longer content with after-the-fact reviews. Instead, we are at the front end of our organizations' strategic undertakings, helping with acquisitions, systems redesign, multinational business expansions, and other initiatives that can mean the difference between success and failure for our clients.

The addition of insight was an important advance for our profession. Yet I believe internal audit's greatest opportunity to add value for its clients lies ahead. That's because we are only now beginning to explore the potential of moving beyond both hindsight and insight—and positioning ourselves to provide foresight.

...To Foresight

For internal auditors, foresight is the ability to peer into the future so we can judge the relative importance of what's ahead for our organization. With it we can help our clients prepare for challenges or opportunities before they even materialize. And foresight can mean the difference between an engagement resulting in another routine audit—or a major success story.

LIFE LESSON #35

Internal auditors deliver a whole new level of added value when they use their knowledge and skills to provide their organizations with foresight that helps management identify and, if necessary, prepare for risks before they even materialize.

Each of us has an innate ability to imagine the future; we do it every day. But foresight is more than just exercising the imagination, interpreting gut feelings, or guessing about future events. No one can perfectly predict the future, but we can work hard to develop the knowledge and skills necessary to understand better what the future may hold.

During my years in client service, I worked with several leading internal audit departments that already delivered real value to their companies by including foresight in their work—whether or not they called it that. For example, the internal audit department of a leading U.S. health-care provider routinely offers advice to its management about risks that could materialize depending on how different scenarios affect health-care legislation and regulations. The auditors weren't recommending which strategies to pursue; they were simply shining an informed, objective light on the future to gauge the hazards that may lie ahead. In my opinion, that is what foresight is all about.

Internal auditors have a strong head start in developing the knowledge and skills needed to demonstrate useful foresight. Pattern recognition, trend assessment, and analysis are second nature to many of us in the profession. Internal auditors also have exceptional opportunities to learn about all aspects of a business, adding depth and focus to our "future view." We tend to look at things with fresh eyes and are trained to challenge existing assumptions and paradigms. In studying past mistakes and current problems, we have become experts at assessing risk and spotting opportunity, which makes us ideal candidates to provide our clients with forward-looking advice as well.

Given that a clear-eyed view of the future requires so many of the skills we use in conducting audits, it seems almost paradoxical that internal auditors are not renowned for their foresight. But just because we possess the tools doesn't mean we know how best to use them when looking forward, rather than into the past. Developing foresight will require hard work. Internal auditors must consciously strive to think in future tense, applying forward-looking analyses to our organizations' strategic plans and operations. Developing these abilities won't guarantee the accuracy of our predictions, but they will mean our foresight will be grounded in the same principles and preparation that have made our hindsight and insight so valuable for so long.

The Trail Ahead

Speaking of foresight, it's a safe bet that the "ideal" internal auditor a few decades from now will be very different from the successful internal auditors working today. The need for our services has never been greater, yet new and more innovative services will be demanded in the future. Because the organizations we serve, and the world in which they operate, are in a constant state of transformation, the internal audit profession must continue to enhance and expand its "portfolio of services" if it is to stay relevant.

Even if we can't predict exactly what will be expected of internal auditors in the future, we can identify many of the things that will continue to make our services valuable. Internal auditors may one day provide previously unimagined forms of assurance, but regardless of the specific services rendered, there will be an ongoing need for independent, objective information and advice. Technology may transform many of our activities, but we must heed the profession's basic principles when serving our stakeholders' needs. The manner in which we provide our services will change, but we must never forget that we are auditing people, not things, and must never forget to demonstrate our value to the organization.

A clearer vision of the future is only the starting point for positive change; not only must we offer strategic foresight to our organizations, we must also help establish a framework and culture for converting that foresight into action. I believe that, above all, the internal auditor of the future will be an agent for positive change.

Regardless of how the lives of future internal auditors might differ from ours, I expect our profession to continue adding value as long as those in it approach their work with open minds and positive attitudes. Attitude is like a paint brush with which you add color to the world. If you have a true passion for the profession, if you cherish your yesterdays and envision bright tomorrows, and if you live every day in full color rather than black and white, I believe you will find internal auditing among the most rewarding jobs on the planet. My sincere hope is that this book provides you not just with new insight into internal auditing, but also with the foresight to propel your journey along the fascinating trail that lies ahead.

NOTES

INTRODUCTION
Lessons Along the Way

1. Merriam-Webster, http://www.merriam-webster.com/
    dictionary/audit%20trail.

CHAPTER 2
Common Traits of Outstanding Internal Auditors

1. IIA Standard 1100: Independence and Objectivity, International
    Professional Practices Framework (IPPF) (Altamonte Springs,
    FL: The Institute of Internal Auditors, 2013).

2. Personal qualities 2–7 and this concluding paragraph were
    adopted from *Internal Auditing: Assurance and Advisory
    Services*, Third Edition (Altamonte Springs, FL: The Institute of
    Internal Auditors Research Foundation, 2013), 1-15–1-16.

CHAPTER 3
No Stakeholders? No Mission

1. The money that becomes available in a national government's
    budget when the country is at peace and can afford to reduce its
    defense spending. The term "peace dividend" is also used to refer
    to an increase in investor confidence that sparks an increase
    in stock prices after a war ends or a major threat to national
    security is eliminated. The money saved from defense spending
    is usually used toward housing, education, and other projects.

2. "Imperatives for Change: The IIA's Global Internal Audit Survey in Action," a component of the CBOK Study, The Institute of Internal Auditors Research Foundation, 2011. Accessed at: http://www .theiia.org/bookstore/product/imperatives-for-change-the-iias -global-internal-audit-survey-in-action-download-pdf-1558.cfm.

CHAPTER 4

The Importance of Value

1. For more information about the Value Proposition, see "Value Proposition: Internal Auditing's Value to Stakeholders" (Altamonte Springs, FL: The Institute of Internal Auditors. Accessed at: https://na.theiia.org/about-us/about-ia/pages/ value-proposition.aspx.

2. Ibid.

3. Rick Telberg, "The Scary New Outlook for Internal Audit," American Institute of Certified Public Accountants, *Career Insider*, April 22, 2010. Accessed at: http://www.cpa2biz. com/Content/media/PRODUCER_CONTENT/Newsletters/ Articles_2010/Career/ScaryOutlook.jsp.

4. Ibid.

5. Ibid.

6. Ibid.

7. "Imperatives for Change: The IIA's Global Internal Audit Survey in Action," a component of the CBOK Study, The Institute of Internal Auditors Research Foundation, 2011. Accessed at: http://www. theiia.org/bookstore/product/imperatives-for-change-the-iias -global-internal-audit-survey-in-action-download-pdf-1558.cfm.

8. This section provides the Executive Summary from The IIA's International Professional Practices Framework (IPPF) Practice Guide, Developing the Internal Audit Strategic Plan. It will be necessary for the internal team to review this entire practice guide and use the information to prepare its own comprehensive strategic plan for meeting the expectations of its stakeholders. The practice guide can be accessed at: http://www.theiia.org/bookstore/downloads/9764013237511/1121_Developing%20IA%20Strategic%20Plan.pdf.

CHAPTER 5

Relationship Acumen Is Essential to Success

1. *Sawyer's Guide for Internal Auditors, Volume 1, Internal Audit Essentials* (Altamonte Springs, FL: The Institute of Internal Auditors Research Foundation, 2013), 139.

2. This section on the relationship triangle was excerpted from *The Broken Triangle*, Deloitte.com. Accessed (November 14, 2013) at: https://www.deloitte.com/assets/Dcom-Uruguay/Local%20Assets/Documents/Auditor%C3%ADa/El%20Tri%C3%A1ngulo%20roto_Auditoria%20Interna_Comite%20de%20auditoria_Gerencia.pdf.

3. Chambers, Eldridge, Park, and Williams. "The Relationship Advantage: Maximizing Chief Audit Executive Success" Korn/Ferry Institute and The IIA Audit Executive Center (March 2011). Accessed November 14, 2013, at: http://www.kornferryinstitute.com/sites/all/files/documents/briefings-magazine-download/%20The%20relationship%20advantage-%20Maximizing%20chief%20audit%20executive%20success%20.pdf.

4. IIA Standard 1111: Direct Interaction With the Board, International Professional Practices Framework (IPPF) (Altamonte Springs, FL: The Institute of Internal Auditors, 2013).

5. This section of relationships with management is quoted from *Sawyer's Guide for Internal Auditors, Volume 1*, 155–156.

6. Daniel Coleman, *Emotional Intelligence* (New York: Bantam, 2012).

7. "The corporate director and succession planning," Korn/Ferry Institute. Accessed at: http://www.kornferryinstitute.com/sites/ all/files//documents/briefings-magazine-download/The% 20corporate%20director%20and%20succession% 20planning%20%E2%80%93%20Nine%20points% 20to%20consider%20when%20preparing%20for%20SEC% 20Bulletin%2014E%20.pdf.

CHAPTER 6

When in Doubt, Follow the Risk

1. Peter Bernstein's examples were cited in *Internal Auditing: Assurance and Advisory Services*, Third Edition (Altamonte Springs, FL: The Institute of Internal Auditors Research Foundation, 2013), 4–2.

2. *Enterprise Risk Management – Integrated Framework*, The Committee of Sponsoring Organizations of the Treadway Commission, 2004.

3. Averages calculated from The IIA Audit Executive Center's spring 2012, 2013, and 2014 Pulse of the Profession surveys of internal audit trends in North America. After 2012, respondents were afforded the opportunity to reflect IT coverage percentages separate from "other." IT coverage has averaged about 11 percent since 2013.

4. Pulse of the Profession 2014, March 2014, The IIA Audit Executive Center.

5. Targeting Key Threats and Changing Expectations to Deliver Greater Value, PricewaterhouseCoopers 2008 State of the Internal Audit Profession Study, April 2008, PricewaterhouseCoopers.

6. Pulse of the Profession 2013: Time to Seize the Opportunity, March 2013, The IIA Audit Executive Center.

7. The Institute of Internal Auditors, Emerging Trends and Leading Practices Survey, Spring 2011.

CHAPTER 7

Risk: A Moving Target

1. Richard J. Anderson and J. Christopher Svare, *Imperatives for Change: The IIA's Global Internal Audit Survey in Action* (Altamonte Springs, FL: The Institute of Internal Auditors Research Foundation), 2011.

2. Ibid.

CHAPTER 8

Communication Must Be Continuous

1. Richard J. Anderson and J. Christopher Svare, *Imperatives for Change: The IIA's Global Internal Audit Survey in Action* (Altamonte Springs, FL: The Institute of Internal Auditors Research Foundation), 2011, 21.

2. "The IIA Global Internal Audit Competency Framework," The Institute of Internal Auditors, 2013. Accessed at: https://na.theiia.org/about-us/Public%20Documents/The%20IIA%20Global%20Internal%20Audit%20Competency%20Framework.pdf.

3. Daniel A. Goble, Lauren E. Shaheen, and Raymond Jeffords, "Questions for Internal Auditors," The Institute of Internal Auditors. Accessed at: https://global.theiia.org/iiarf/Public%20Documents/Questions%20for%20Internal%20Auditors%20%20-%20Chattanooga.pdf.

4. IIA Practice Guide, Interaction with the Board, August 2011, The Institute of Internal Auditors. Accessed at: https://na.theiia.org/standards-guidance/Member%20Documents/11759_PROF-Interaction_with_the_Board_PG.pdf.

CHAPTER 9

Planning, the Most Important Phase of an Engagement

1. IIA Practice Advisory 2210.A1-1, Risk Assessment in Engagement Planning, International Professional Practices Framework (IPPF) (Altamonte Springs, FL: The Institute of Internal Auditors, 2013).

2. Ibid.

3. Ronell B. Raaum and Stephen L Morgan, *Performance Auditing: A Measurement Approach*, 2nd Edition (Altamonte Springs, FL: The Institute of Internal Auditors Research Foundation, 2009).

4. IIA Practice Advisory 2410-1: Communication Criteria, International Professional Practices Framework (IPPF) (Altamonte Springs, FL: The Institute of Internal Auditors, 2013).

5. IIA Practice Advisory 2200-1: Engagement Planning, International Professional Practices Framework (IPPF) (Altamonte Springs, FL: The Institute of Internal Auditors, 2013).

6. *Internal Auditing: Assurance and Advisory Services,* Third Edition (Altamonte Springs, FL: The Institute of Internal Auditors Research Foundation, 2013), 12-3–12-5.

CHAPTER 10

Fight the Temptation to Over-Audit

1. IIA Standard 2300: Performing the Engagement, International Professional Practices Framework (IPPF) (Altamonte Springs, FL: The Institute of Internal Auditors, 2013).

2. *Sawyer's Guide for Internal Auditors, Volume 1, Internal Audit Essentials* (Altamonte Springs, FL: The Institute of Internal Auditors Research Foundation, 2013), 186.

3. IIA Standard 2310: Identifying Information, International Professional Practices Framework (IPPF) (Altamonte Springs, FL: The Institute of Internal Auditors, 2013).

4. Government Auditing Standards, Paragraph 6.79, "Audit Documentation," 2011, The Comptroller General of the United States, The Government Accountability Office, Washington, DC.

5. The IIA Audit Executive Center, "Technology Laggers vs. Embracers: CAEs Discuss Technology Performance Gap," white paper (September 2012).

6. *The IIA CIA Learning System, Part IV* (Altamonte Springs, FL: The Institute of Internal Auditors, 2007), 64.

Chapter 11

Internal Audit Reporting: The Ultimate Obstacle to Timeliness

1. Lawrence B. Sawyer, Mortimer A. Dittenhofer, James H. Scheiner, *Sawyer's Internal Auditing: The Practice of Modern Internal Auditing*, 5th Edition (Altamonte Springs, FL: The Institute of Internal Auditors, 2003), 690.

Chapter 12

Innovation Drives Greatness

1. Brian Loughman, "Overcoming the Disparity Between Policy and Practice as it Relates to Fraud," *Corporate Compliance Insights,* October 28, 2013. Accessed at: http://www.corporatecomplianceinsights.com/overcoming-the-disparity-between-policy-and-practice-as-it-relates-to-fraud/.

2. *Internal Auditing: Assurance and Advisory Services*, Third Edition (Altamonte Springs, FL: The Institute of Internal Auditors Research Foundation, 2013).

3. Kathy Chin Leong, December 27, 2013, comment on Gopi Kallayil, "Google Reveals Its 9 Principles of Innovation," Fast Company.com blog, 2013. Accessed at: http://www.fastcompany.com/3021956/how-to-be-a-success-at-everything/googles-nine-principles-of-innovation.

4. This section on Innovation Behaviors is adapted from "How can innovation transform internal audit?" PricewaterhouseCoopers, 2009. Accessed at: http://www.pwc.com.au/assurance/assets/ Innovation-Internal-Audit-Nov09.pdf.

5. Glen L. Gray and Maryann Jacobi Gray, *Enhancing Internal Auditing Through Innovative Practices* (Altamonte Springs, FL: The Institute of Internal Auditors, 1996).

6. This section on common challenges in implementing innovations is adapted from Glen L. Gray and Maryann Jacobi Gray, *Enhancing Internal Auditing Through Innovative Practices*, 7–17.

CHAPTER 13

Small Stones Can Cause the Biggest Waves

1. "The case for the $435 hammer," *TheFreeLibrary*. Accessed at: http://www.thefreelibrary.com/ The+case+for+the+$435+hammer.-a04619906.

2. "Navy investigating bills for $660 ashtrays, $400 wrenches," *Associated Press*, May 28, 1985. Accessed at: http://www.apnewsarchive.com/1985/Navy -Investigating-Bills-For-$660-Ashtrays-$400-Wrenches/ id-24fa49472f8896be342ea5fac09c8a4a.

3. "Project on Government Oversight," *Wikipedia*. Accessed at: http://en.wikipedia.org/wiki/Project_On_Government _Oversight.

4. Azeezaly S. Jaffer, Manager Stamp Services, "Review of the Printing Error in the Grand Canyon Stamp (RG-LA-99-001)." Accessed at: http://www.uspsoig.gov/sites/default/files/ document-library-files/2013/rg-la-99-001.pdf.

5. Information adapted from Richard Powelson, "TVA workers reprimanded for alien search," June 18, 2001, *InfoSec News*. Accessed at: http://www.nandotimes.com/technology/story/28884p-501336c.html; and P. Vasishtha, "IG slams ET search," June 22, 2001, *GNC.com*. Accessed at: http://gcn.com/articles/2001/06/22/ig-slams-et-search.aspx.

6. Andy Sher, "TVA identifies lavish spending," *The Chattanooga Free Times*, May 3, 2001.

7. Richard Powelson, "TVA Nashville to Downsize Space," *The Knoxville News Sentinel*, July 19, 2002.

CHAPTER 14

No One Is Immune to Ethical Lapses

1. Howard Sklar, "Infernal Audit: When Internal Auditors Go Bad," February 24, 2012. Accessed at: http://www.forbes.com/sites/howardsklar/2012/02/24/quis-custodiet-ipsos-custodes/.

2. International Professional Practices Framework (IPPF) (Altamonte Springs, FL: The Institute of Internal Auditors, 2013), 4–6.

3. Max H. Bazerman and Ann E. Tenbrunsel, *Blind Spots* (Princeton, NJ: Princeton University Press, 2012).

4. Cynthia Cooper, *Extraordinary Circumstances* (Hoboken, NJ: John Wiley & Sons, 2009).

5. Ibid.

6. IIA Standard 1312: External Assessments, International Professional Practices Framework (IPPF) (Altamonte Springs, FL: The Institute of Internal Auditors, 2013).

7. Emily N. Strauss, "'Easing Out' the FCPA Facilitation Payment Exception," I.C.1: "The Facilitation Payment Exception," page 241. Accessed at: http://www.bu.edu/law/central/ jd/organizations/journals/bulr/volume92n4/documents/ STRAUSS.pdf.

8. Cynthia Cooper, *Extraordinary Circumstances*.

CHAPTER 15

Always Remember—We Are Auditing People Too

1. "Fraud Detection and Prevention," The Institute of Internal Auditors Ottawa Chapter. Accessed at: https://chapters.theiia. org/ottawa/Documents/Fraud_Detection_and_Prevention.pdf.

2. "Report to the Nations on Occupational Fraud and Abuse," 2012 Global Fraud Study, *The Association of Certified Fraud Examiners*. Accessed at: http://www.acfe.com/uploadedFiles/ ACFE_Website/Content/rttn/2012-report-to-nations.pdf.

3. Ibid.

4. International Professional Practices Framework (IPPF) (Altamonte Springs, FL: The Institute of Internal Auditors, 2013), 43.

5. Michael Capote and Cecil Greek, "Theorist Paper: Donald Cressey." Accessed at: criminology.fsu.edu/crimtheory/2004/ Cressey.doc.

6. Ryan Hubbs, "Fraud brainstorming," *Fraud Magazine*, July/ August 2012. Accessed at: http://www.fraud-magazine.com/ article.aspx?id=4294973852.

7.   International Professional Practices Framework (IPPF) (Altamonte Springs, FL: The Institute of Internal Auditors, 2013), 20.

8.   IIA Practice Guide, Internal Auditing and Fraud, December 2009, The Institute of Internal Auditors. Accessed at: https://na.theiia.org/standards-guidance/recommended-guidance/practice-guides/Pages/Internal-Auditing-and-Fraud-Practice-Guide.aspx.

9.   Rudyard Kipling, "If," quoted in *Kipling: Poems* (New York: Everyman's Library, 2007).